GOOD
FOOD
FOR MEN

Gabriel Gaté's

GOOD
FOOD
FOR MEN

Photography by John Hay

WHA

First published in 1996 by William Heinemann Australia
a part of Reed Books Australia
22 Salmon Street, Port Melbourne, Victoria 3207
a division of Reed International Books Australia Pty Ltd

Compiling editor Angie Burns Gaté
Edited by Foong Ling Kong
Designed and illustrated by Luisa Laino
Food styling by Gabriel Gaté and John Hay
Typeset by Luisa Laino
Printed and bound by Southbank

National Library of Australia
        cataloguing-in-publication data:
        Gaté, Gabriel, 1955- .
        Gabriel Gaté's good food for men.

        Includes index.
        ISBN 0 85561 715 2.

        1. Cookery. I. Title

641.5

FoReWoRd

My mother is a wonderful cook and my culinary education began at her side half a century ago. Our meals often began with soup, followed by meat and three veg and hot pudding in winter, and meat, salad and home-made ice-cream in summer. However, she has never stopped experimenting and I have followed her example. *Gabriel Gaté's Family Food* and *Smart Food* were my sons' first cookery books, and also my favourites during the last decade. It gives me, therefore, special pleasure to introduce *Good Food for Men*.

I love food, especially meals with a variety of colours, aromas, textures and tastes. But most of all I enjoy preparing these meals and sharing them with my family and friends over a glass of good wine. As a child, I learned to prepare and cook food and I have taught both my sons to enjoy shopping for food and creating meals (which they consume with relish!).

Gabriel offers a 'recipe' for a more enjoyable life. Shop for the ingredients for meals that you love. Visit the local market and shops with your friends and family, or take time out for yourself to buy your favourite foodstuffs. Remember to set time aside – this should be a relaxed, enjoyable experience perhaps punctuated by conversation over coffee and lively discourse with the shopkeepers or your companions. Likewise, when you prepare your favourite meals consider when it can be a social occasion and when it should be a solo creation.

Gabriel's new book continues the tradition he has established with the Anti-Cancer Council of Victoria; encouraging us to enjoy our food and eat for health at the same time. *Good Food for Men* is for everyone; it will show you how you can reduce your risk of cancer and heart disease and add to your enjoyment of life. You should be slimmer, fitter and happier if you combine the healthy diet described in *Good Food for Men* with regular exercise and avoidance of tobacco. This is a book for all *bons vivants. Bon appetit!*

Dr Robert Burton
Director, Anti-Cancer Council of Victoria

Acknowledgments

Most of all I would like to thank my wife, Angie, for her support and assistance in writing this book. I am grateful for the endorsement given to the book by the Anti-Cancer Council of Victoria and wish to thank its Director, Dr Robert Burton, and all his staff, in particular Dr David Hill, Graham Giles and Paul Ireland for their advice on nutrition and diet. It was a joy to work with Adrian Collette and his team at Reed Books. Thanks go to Sue Hines, the driving force behind the book, and to John Hay, Kirsten Alexander, Foong Ling Kong, Luisa Laino, Julie Pinkham and Rod Howard. Thanks also to my sons, Sebastian and Michael, and to the many friends who helped in various ways, especially Janet Wang for her advice on Asian food, Terry Greguol and Mario Russo from Mario's greengrocer, Henrique Godinho of Casa Portuguesa, Jonathan Gianfreda of Jonathan's of Collingwood, Gianni Omizzolo from Donnini's Pasta, Kusum-Chhotu of Bombay Bazaar, all at Claringbold's Fish Shop and to many others at the Prahran Market. My grateful thanks to our staff at the Gabriel Gaté Cookware Shop in Hawthorn, in particular Robyn Campbell-Wood. Lastly, thanks to all the men who helped by answering my questionnaire.

What this Book will do for You

When I first started work on *Good Food for Men* I was encouraged by the interest my project aroused among my male and female friends. The title itself stimulated much discussion and the questions most often asked were 'What's the difference between food for men and food for women?' and 'Isn't the title a little bit sexist?'.

Not being able to cook has been a problem for too many men and women for too long. In all my time cooking and teaching I have also observed that, generally, men don't have as good a knowledge as women when it comes to food, just as boys are not encouraged to contribute to the family cooking the way girls are. Men love to eat, but they do less food shopping and cooking than women. In my own cooking classes, which are open to both sexes, there is, on average, one man for every ten women. Ultimately the choices men make in regard to food, health and independence are affected by this lack of culinary experience and knowledge.

Good Food for Men will serve many functions. The first and most important is that it be used by both men and women as a guide to cooking and eating for well-being. The second, and closer to my heart, is that it will encourage men to cook for themselves for pleasure and independence. The third is that it can help both men and women become better cooks. Cooking is a wonderful skill and being able to cook is a source of great sensual pleasure, a social asset, and a splendid way to boost self-esteem.

I urge you to read the sections on Cooking and Eating for Well-being (p. 28) and How to Become a Good Cook (p. 2) before you start. By the time you have read them you will have already become a better cook.

If you love delicious food, wish to enjoy long-lasting health and possess a secret desire to become a good cook, and if you want to know what food is best for all members of your family, then this book is for you.

Best wishes, and happy cooking!
Gabriel Gaté

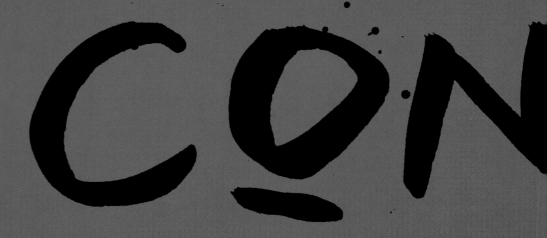CON

tENts

introd

uction

HOW to become A Good COOK

The skills of good cooking can be learnt by anybody, and as with most skills, the younger you learn the easier it is. However, the task of learning as an adult can be made easier if you draw on your past experience, observations and cultural background. You will progress more quickly if you cook regularly and practise new dishes that introduce you to new foods, new seasonings and new techniques, and you will be further encouraged if you buy the best fresh foods you can afford. Try not to become disheartened by occasional failures – you can learn as much from them as from your successes. And you will have many successes. Cooking is one of the only crafts in which even a novice can create something marvellous! Share your knowledge and learn from more experienced cooks around you.

Encourage your teenage children to cook and share your knowledge with them.

MeMORise YOUR EXPeRieNCE

Memory is a most important asset in cooking. It is the guardian of our experience. While shopping, try to take in all aspects of as many foods as you can. An acute and well-trained sense of smell and taste, for instance, will help you ascertain the freshness of meat, fish and vegetables.

Smelling

Smelling plant foods must be one of the greatest pleasures we can indulge in. Think of the wonderful aromas of basil, mango, ginger, peach, cummin, rosemary, mandarin, lavender, lemon and coffee. When you smell a peach, for example, your experience will tell you if the peach is at its best or not. If that peach is the best one you have ever smelt, that smell will take the place of honour in your memory cells and become the model. Try recording the smells of certain liquids, such as oils (walnut, olive, corn), vinegars, wines, liqueurs, bottled sauces and so on. The more you allow your sense of smell to develop, the easier it is to differentiate between good and mediocre food. When you cook, the aromas coming from your pots, pans and oven also carry messages. An experienced cook will be able to interpret those messages perfectly. For example, an Italian cook can smell when the bolognese sauce is cooked; a baker can tell when the bread is ready to come out of the oven just by smelling it.

Touching

You also need to develop a very subtle sense of touch to become a good cook. Cooking is a gentle craft, and it is always a great spectacle to watch a good cook choose, prepare, and cook fresh ingredients. With experience, your sense of touch will help you select food and assess its texture, maturity and ripeness. At every stage your hands play a major role in the process of food preparation, so do not be afraid to use them; it would certainly be difficult to choose an avocado without touching it. Your hands also perform the manual cooking tasks like slicing, cutting and chopping, so practise using kitchen implements such as a knife properly, and try to master new cutting techniques. Practice will also help you get a feel for the ingredients.

Looking

Our sense of sight plays an invaluable part in every aspect of food preparation, especially during the cooking process, in anticipating the changes that occur to food as it cooks. We often underestimate the knowledge that we gain from focusing on our cooking or from watching others cook. I assure you that these accumulated experiences will make you a better cook.

Focus carefully on what you buy.
Teach yourself to choose the best
and freshest produce.

Tasting and Texture

Likewise, take every opportunity to taste food, especially new foods, and smell foods when they are in season (and therefore at their best) to refresh your memory. When tasting, think of the flavours. Is it sweet, salty, sour, acidic or a mixture?

And what of the textures? Our lips, mouth and tongue are extremely sensitive and thrill at the various components in a dish. In some dishes the texture of the ingredients is as important as the taste.

Think of the softness of ice-cream, or the hot potato chip, which is crisp on the outside and soft on the inside. Think of a mixed salad of crisp leaves, crunchy nuts, melt-in-the-mouth avocado and an oily, slippery dressing. You'll be surprised how your cooking can improve when you pay attention to contrasting textures as well as flavour.

Texture can be controlled in several ways. One is in the ingredients you choose. Certain ingredients simply need to be cut in a different style to offer a different texture. Think of the difference between grated carrot and small carrot sticks, between finely shredded lettuce and whole leaves. Cooking methods or techniques also control texture. To my taste, for example, a carrot purée served with a grilled steak is more exciting than steamed whole carrots. Look at some of the photographs in this book and consider the ways in which the various textures of the ingredients contribute to the enjoyment of a dish. Next time you visit your favourite restaurant, take note of all the little things the chef has added to stimulate your senses and palate – it may be the egg, nuts, herbs, vegetables cut in different ways, olives, seeds or fruit.

When you like a particular preparation, try to find out its ingredients and memorise them if possible. The memory of a wide range of tastes and textures will give you the same freedom in your cooking that a musician has when playing without the written music.

COOKING WITH BOTH SIDES OF THE BRAIN

It is now recognised by experts that the right and left sides of the brain have different functions. The right side of the brain is associated with imagination, artistry, music and creativity, while the left side is linked to logic, planning and organisation.

Applied to the kitchen this means that the right side of the brain is the creative cook while the left side is the efficient organiser and cleaner. So when preparing a meal, those who use only the right side of their brain usually prepare beautiful food but leave behind a big mess (and get into trouble with the people they live with!). Others who overwork the left side of their brain have a spotless kitchen but the cooking is usually not too great, for they focus more on the cleaning up than the cooking.

Do you recognise yourself somewhere here? The lucky ones are those whose right and left sides of the brain complement one another. Experts on the subject of brain power tend to agree that it would be best to allow each side of the brain to take turns, as the two sides don't seem to work well at the same time – it is a bit like two people speaking simultaneously.

When you want to be creative while cooking, stopping every two minutes to clean can cause the creative flow to disappear and you lose interest. From my experience, people who do not really enjoy cooking are affected by the left side of their brain, which overpowers the right. Experienced writers know that one cannot write creatively (right brain) and edit (left brain) at the same time. The improvement and editing come *after* the writing.

In the preparation of meals the process is similar. Once you have planned what to cook and have bought your ingredients, the left side of the brain gets into gear. You tidy up your workbench and read your recipe carefully; you prepare your equipment; sort out the ingredients and do the peeling and cleaning jobs. Then, when all of the preparation is done and the ingredients are assembled, the left side of the brain can rest and allow the right side to focus on the wonderful task of making the dish.

So don't let the left side nag you while you concentrate. Get rid of distractions such as the television, phone calls and heavy discussions. Let your mind be with the dish, otherwise the pleasures of cooking will be diminished. After you have enjoyed your meal, let the left side of the brain get back to work to look after the cleaning. And when several people live together it is a bonus if everyone shares the cleaning tasks.

Next time you prepare a meal, try to become more aware of when the left and right sides of your brain are functioning. It is quite fun, really.

LEARNING to COOK A NEW DISH

Whether you are a novice or experienced cook, the easiest way to become a better cook is to learn new dishes. Cooking a new dish introduces you to new ingredients, new seasonings, new techniques, and, sometimes, new cookware. As you become more confident and experienced, move on to more challenging or involved recipes. When you start learning choose a simple dish to cook, such as a soup, salad, pasta or fruit salad. And remember that even when cooking for others, it is best to prepare a dish you would enjoy eating yourself; it is difficult to become enthusiastic about cooking something you dislike.

In this book you will find many simple dishes to try. You can also try your hand at familiar dishes you like, such as those your parents or friends have cooked for you in the past. I highly recommend selecting something you have either seen demonstrated on television or featured in a magazine or cookbook. Having prior knowledge about the dish gives you more confidence and direction, whereas attempting a recipe you know nothing about is a bit like walking in the dark. Avoid cooking more than one new dish at a time. Take it slowly, for a new experience can be mentally and physically trying.

Once you have the written recipe in hand, read it all the way through carefully to work out a few things. First, are the ingredients available and in season? You can't get figs in spring but you might be able to substitute cherries or the first of the stone fruits. A certain type of fish or vegetable in a recipe can be easily substituted for another, according to the season. Make sure you have the necessary equipment and try to understand and work through the various steps of the recipe.

Try the following mental exercise:

Imagine breaking 3 eggs into a medium-sized glass bowl. Season with a small pinch of salt, a little freshly ground black pepper and 1 tablespoon chopped parsley. Using a hand whisk, mix in 1 cup of milk, whisking for 10 seconds until the preparation becomes runny.

For a change, prepare a pasta dish you've never tried before.

Performing this exercise will help you understand how important it is to concentrate when you read a recipe. By the time you have finished reading, you ought to have an idea of the

steps involved and approximately how long it will take to prepare the dish. Remember that the time indicated in a recipe is only a guide, and that it almost always takes longer on the first try.

Carefully choose the day you intend to cook your dish, and take into consideration the time required for the shopping, the preparation and the cooking. Avoid days when you may be tired, rushed or distracted. In this way, you can plan for the experience to be a pleasant one.

Prepare a detailed shopping list (p. 12) and check your pantry, refrigerator or freezer to see which ingredients and seasonings you already have, checking their use-by dates as well. Organise the order in which to do your shopping. First buy the least perishable foods, such as potatoes and pumpkin, followed by more perishable items, such as fish and dairy foods. When shopping on a hot day, try to park your car in the shade and avoid leaving delicate ingredients in a hot car for too long. If the weather is very hot, it is a good idea to have an esky in the boot.

Just before beginning to cook, read the whole recipe through carefully. Avoid rushing, and try to concentrate calmly on the task. Your first attempt at a dish may be a great success and, whether pleased or not with the result, you will have learnt a lot and be on the way to becoming a better cook. While cooking, take notes – perhaps the pan got too hot during cooking or the cake took another 10 minutes in your oven – they will be of great help to you the next time you try the dish.

I can't stress enough how important it is to cook the same dish at least once or twice again soon after, in order to build on what you have learnt and to memorise the experience. There have been many times when I have been not quite satisfied with my first attempt, but I only feel that I fail if I give up then. The second time around is so much easier, and by the third the experience is a pleasure. You will see that practice makes a huge difference.

Imagine how much better a cook you can become if you give yourself the easy task of learning a new dish or two a month. Mark off the days in your diary when you will cook your next three or four new dishes and write the names of the recipes in the calendar.

The Art of Having Everything Ready at the Same Time

In cooking, as in music, timing is all important. You want all the elements of a meal (vegetables, fish or meat, pasta, rice, potatoes) to be ready at about the same time. Before starting to cook, take time to think. Quickly rehearse in your mind the various steps in the preparation and establish the order of doing things. Sometimes a recipe may suggest a particular order that does not suit you because you lack the ideal equipment, so you may need to reconsider how you will go about it.

Remember that you can keep many foods warm for a little while in a very low oven at 100°C (210°F). Just cover the food with foil to stop it from drying out. Vegetables can be kept warm in a steamer with the heat turned off and the lid on, and foods can be reheated briefly in the microwave. When you cook a dish of pan-fried or grilled meat or fish with vegetables, start cooking the vegetables first so as to have them ready just before the meat or fish. When cooking a large roast, such as a leg of lamb, begin by cooking the meat first, followed by the roast vegetables, and lastly, the greens. However, for a small roast that takes less than 30 minutes to cook, start by roasting the vegetables first.

For pasta dishes, make sure the sauce is made before you put on the pasta. For stir-fry dishes, do all the cutting before starting to cook, and in most cases, stir-fry the vegetables separately before the meat. When noodles are served with a stir-fry dish, cook them first and then mix with the vegetables and meat. When serving a salad with a quick meal, prepare the salad leaves and dressing first; toss them together only at the last minute.

Most casserole dishes and soups can be prepared several hours, or even a day or two, in advance. They will taste better, too, if the flavours are allowed to mature. Avoid leaving the cooking of such dishes until the last moment as they can take longer than anticipated.

Most vegetables take between 8 and 15 minutes to cook if you are steaming, and a little less if boiling. Dry pasta takes 9 to 12 minutes to cook; fresh pasta requires less time. White rice needs about 17 to 20 minutes, while brown rice takes 35 to 40 minutes. Pan-fried or grilled steak takes 5 to 10 minutes. A pan-fried chicken fillet takes between 8 and 15 minutes. A roasted leg of lamb takes 45 minutes to 1 hour in an oven at 180°C (350°F). A medium roast chicken takes 45 minutes to 1 hour in a 180°C (350°F) oven. Roast beef takes about 35 minutes per kilogram in a 180°C (350°F) oven. In the same oven a chicken casserole takes 30 to 40 minutes, while a beef casserole needs 1 to 2 hours.

When you cook for a large number, ask for help in serving the food. That way everyone will be able to enjoy and share in the meal.

Discover the Magic of Herbs and Spices

The intensity of flavour in herbs and spices can change a rather bland dish into a master-piece in seconds. Supermarkets these days offer a choice of dozens of spices, and any good greengrocer will have at least half a dozen varieties of fresh herbs all year round. To become familiar with herbs and spices, use them one at a time in your cooking so you can learn, and memorise, their flavours. For example, start by adding a little sliced basil to pasta or over some sliced tomato, or by using ginger in your next stir-fry. Once you know the individual flavours, and which goes best with what, you can then blend them. Most traditional ethnic foods have the distinctive flavours of certain herbs, spices and seasonings – try to see if you can taste them the next time you visit a restaurant or try out a new dish.

Following are some of the flavours you might encounter:

Greece	Olive oil, lemon, oregano
Italy, France	Olive oil, garlic, basil or parsley
South of France	Olive oil, thyme, tomato, garlic
Hungary	Onion, paprika
Mexico	Tomato, chilli
Spain	Olive oil, onion, tomato, saffron
North Africa	Tomato, cummin, chilli, coriander, cinnamon, olive oil
India	Onion, garlic, ginger, curry spice mix
Thailand	Fish sauce, spices, chilli, lemongrass, coriander
China	Ginger, garlic, soy sauce, rice wine

It is a common belief that the more spices or herbs used in a dish, the better it will taste. This is not true. Learn to use herbs and spices, but in moderation, so that you preserve the special quality and natural flavour of the food you are seasoning. In the interests of freshness, it is essential to replace your supply of ground spices at least every six months.

Although herbs and spices have been used in cooking and medicine for over 5000 years, there is still much to discover about their virtues. Many herbs and spices assist in the production of saliva and so contribute to an improved digestion. Recent studies have found that herbs belonging to the onion family such as garlic, onion, shallots and chives might help prevent certain cancers, while others such as coriander, fenugreek and onion are thought to be beneficial for those suffering from diabetes. Some, such as garlic, cloves, mustard and horseradish, have antiseptic properties and might slow down or stop the development of certain bacteria. Cloves, pepper, turmeric, ginger, nutmeg, sage and rosemary have antioxidant properties. Chillies vary in heat and intensity from the very mild to very hot, but need to be used in moderation as they can irritate the digestive system.

Many of the recipes in this book use herbs and spices, and you may enjoy keeping a few herbs in pots or in the garden to enhance your cooking. By getting to know the qualities of herbs and spices and using them for seasoning, you will learn to effectively cut down on the use of salt and oil in your cooking.

Notebooks

A notebook is a great learning aid and help to a cook. In her kitchen notebook, my wife, Angie, had jotted down recipes I cooked when we first met twenty years ago. If she hadn't done this, we would have forgotten some of our favourite dishes of the time. In my own notebook I have recorded some favourite recipes handed down by my mother and grandmother, as well as many dishes I have learnt in my travels and in my work as a chef. Most of them are now filed in a computer. In addition to actual recipes, I also record any special thoughts I may have, and ideas for different seasonings, cookery techniques, seasonal and special occasion menus and so on.

All this recorded knowledge may be of interest to relatives and friends. Many young men and women would value learning to cook from a more experienced cook, and I think our modern society could gain much from going back to the former tradition of passing on cooking knowledge from one generation to another. If the school curriculum taught young children the pleasures of developing their senses of smell, taste, touch and sight in relation to food, young people would be in a position to make better food choices, especially when also encouraged to contribute to family meals from an early age at home.

Shop for Fresh Food about Three Times a Week

The concept of one-stop shopping once a week has been promoted as highly convenient. I must admit I particularly dislike this idea for several reasons. First, shopping once a week forces you to plan what you are going to eat a long time in advance. Often it's far too much ahead. It is simply not exciting to know what you will eat in six days' time. By shopping once a week you are also forced to eat food that is not fresh for at least half of your meals. This is far from ideal. Sure, most of the grocery shopping can be done once weekly, but try to buy fresh food at least three times a week.

Following are some guidelines to remember. Eat fish, seafood and minced meat dishes or very thinly cut meats on the day you buy them. Meat cuts such as steak, chops and portioned chicken are best consumed within two days. Cook roasts within two to three days. The general rule is, the bigger the joint of meat, the longer it keeps. Buy vegetables and fruits three times a week – the fresher they are, the more nutritious they will be.

To my way of thinking, the freezing of fresh seafood and meats is necessary only when there is no alternative. Fresh is best.

Shopping lists

One of my favourite moments in the preparation of a meal is the time just before the cooking, when all the ingredients are assembled before me and I feel happy with them. On the other hand, everyone knows how frustrating it is to be ready to begin cooking and then realise that an important ingredient is missing.

A shopping list is of great help, and it is worthwhile including as much detail as you can to facilitate the shopping later. I prefer to write my list from my kitchen, where I can

Nuts and pulses are a
good source of protein.

check what I need for the pantry, fridge and freezer. Even if you can't make up your mind on what you want to eat, it is still essential to check the pantry and fridge for basics such as oil, rice, spices and so on; then you can decide on your meal when at the market or shops. When I visit a market I have a good look first and sometimes sit down to finish my shopping list before actually buying anything.

At the top of the list I write a few important reminders like the fruits I need for the fruit bowl or the name of a particular dish. Then I make three or four columns with headings under groceries, fruit and vegetables, meat and fish and miscellaneous. Here is an example:

Breakfast food

Fruit for the fruit bowl

Sandwich fillings

Fish and green vegetables

Chicken and Vegetable Soup (for Saturday)

Pear and Prune Loaf (for Sunday)

Birthday cake for Michael

Groceries

muesli

skim milk

self-raising flour

peanut butter

½ cup almond meal

cinnamon powder

10 dried pear halves

10 dried apricots

20 dried prunes

4 dried apple rings

long-grain rice

cloves

olive oil

6 eggs

tuna in oil

Fruit & Veg

3 grapefruits

6 bananas

1 lemon

4 apples

2 pears

4 oranges

1 mango

½ kg broccoli

1 kg carrots (medium)

1 leek (medium)

1 bunch parsley

1 bunch lemon thyme

1 head garlic

green salad

1 avocado

1 brown onion

2 tomatoes

Meat & Fish

2 fish cutlets

1 chicken (1.2 kg)

Misc

foil

baking paper

Baker

cake

bread

When cooking from a recipe such as the Pear and Prune Loaf that calls for 10 dried pear halves, 10 dried apricots and so on, you may have to buy more than you need, as dried fruits are often sold according to weight.

My list is just an example, and you'll enjoy making your list in your own style.

Visit a market for inspiration and knowledge

At the age of sixteen, I was lucky enough to be apprenticed to an extraordinary master chef, Albert Augereau, who took me several times a week to the Saumur market in the region of Anjou. He taught me the importance of smelling foods, touching them with respect and focusing on them to really see their beauty. Today I often take my cookery students to the market where they, too, can learn to recognise fresh produce, which is the backbone of a good dish. Just as visitors to an art gallery stand enthralled before a beautiful still-life painting, our senses are unconsciously stimulated in much the same way each time we visit a fresh food market. Just picture peaches, mangoes, cherries, strawberries, asparagus, bok choy and hundreds of other foods of all shapes, sizes, smells, textures and colours – they bombard our senses and interact with our brains.

When you visit a market you will be inspired to create meals from the available fresh, seasonal produce or dream of a new dish altogether. When I arrive at the market, I first stroll through the aisles, making a mental note of who has the best and most reasonably priced product. I don't hesitate to stop at a stall and closely inspect the ingredients before making up my mind.

Learn to recognise the best food suppliers

All food storekeepers, whether they be butchers, fishmongers, bakers or greengrocers, work very hard for many hours each week. The most dedicated greengrocers and fishmongers must be up in the early hours of the morning to get the best produce at the wholesale markets. They also have to establish and maintain a good network of contacts to ensure that they get a regular supply of first-rate produce. The best suppliers are busy, give good service and advice, and have a large turnover so the food is always fresh. There are, however, some busy stores with fast turnover and low prices which unfortunately sell food of an inferior quality, so you need to be vigilant.

To recognise quality and freshness requires practice. As an exercise, I suggest that you stop for a few minutes and have a good look at the display each time you pass a butcher, fishmonger or greengrocer. At the greengrocer's, look at the firmness and quality of the vegetables. Are the carrots unblemished? Is the cauliflower white? Are the greens limp? What herbs are on sale? Is the fruit carefully displayed? Look at the bananas. Are they a nice yellow colour, unblemished and just ripe? Or are they all green or over-ripe? Smell the fruits for sweetness and ripeness. Inspect the red fruits

1 Food mixer	7 Grater	14 Cast-iron grill	22 Conical strainer
2 Egg slide	8 Sharpening steel	15 Blender	23 Pepper grinder
3 Pasta lifter	9 Knives	16 Whisk	24 Scales
4 Skimmer	10 Oven rack	17 Serving spoon	25 Food processor
5 Flat oven tray	11 Roasting tray	18 Colander	26 Measuring jug
6 Multifunction saucepan: stockpot, steamer, pasta cooker	12 Wooden chopping board	19 Wooden tongs	27 Wooden spoon
	13 Pastry cutter and PVC pipe	20 Non-stick frying pan	28 Food mill (mouli)
		21 Casserole dish	29 Wok

Kitchen Equipment

The saying 'a craftsperson is only as good as his or her tools' is most applicable to cooking. Good cookware is of enormous benefit to any cook and helps save time, effort and, in the long run, money. My advice is to buy the best cookware you can afford; you won't regret investing in the things you need in the kitchen. If you cannot afford equipment that is used only occasionally, try borrowing it from family and friends.

The photograph on the opposite page shows a selection of recommended kitchen equipment. If you are just beginning to cook, don't feel you have to have everything. Start off with the basics: a few pans (large and small), a knife or two, a chopping board and a few small pieces of equipment, such as a strainer and wooden spoons.

Knives

Good knives are a cook's best friends. A good knife has balance between the blade and the handle, and a weight you are comfortable with. Ask for advice on how to store knives properly and how to take care of them. Chef's knives are usually the best to buy, and when you cook every day they are more than an indulgence. To do all kinds of small jobs, such as peeling and trimming fruits and vegetables, you will need a small paring knife with a blade of about 10 cm (4 in). A medium–sized knife with a wide blade about 20 cm (8 in) long is perfect for cutting vegetables and other foods. A boning knife has a thin but strong blade about 15 cm (6 in) long, and is useful for trimming fat from meat, portioning chicken and cutting fish into pieces. A serrated knife is useful for cutting bread and other slicing work. The good news is there will soon be good-quality knives on the market that require no sharpening. But in the meantime, to keep your knives sharp, you will need a sharpening steel.

Saucepans and frying pans

Buy the best saucepans you can afford and don't feel you need a complete set as there are sizes you may never use. Buy them individually and select pans with well-fitting lids. For low-fat cooking, non-stick cookware is highly recommended and the most useful pieces are a frying pan and a wide saucepan or casserole dish for casseroles and soups. A large stainless-steel steamer is terrific for cooking vegetables and can also be used to cook pasta, rice, soups and stocks.

Baking dishes, oven racks and grills

For roasting meat or baking, get a large, deep oven tray, preferably a heavy one so you can use it on top of the stove as well. An oven rack that fits into the roasting tray will allow the heat to circulate well around the food being roasted. A flat oven tray with a small edge is useful for baking fish fillets and vegetables. A cast-iron grill is perfect for grilling meat, fish and vegetables on top of the stove and can also be used in the oven.

Woks

What a fabulous cooking utensil the wok is! It can be used for stir-frying, boiling, steaming, casseroles, curries, soups and more. It is one of the best utensils to buy, and good value for money. Choose a thin but robust iron wok with a lid. The wok should come with a stir-fry spatula.

Food mixers, food processors and blenders, juicers, food mills and graters

An electric food mixer with a large metal bowl usually comes with three basic attachments: a balloon whisk, a beater and a dough hook. This piece of equipment makes bread, pizza dough, pastry, cakes and so on. Some food mixers offer other attachments such as a mincer, pasta maker or citrus juicer.

An electric food processor is another useful tool and offers several attachments for slicing and grating foods as well as one or more blades to mix, chop, blend or purée food.

An electric blender is ideal for blending soups into purées or just blending a liquid preparation. An electric juicer turns fruits and vegetables into superb drinks. A food mill (or vegetable mouli) is a hand-operated kitchen gadget for blending or puréeing food. It is good for soups and purées, and the best utensil for making mashed potato. A hand grater is essential for grating carrots, cabbage for coleslaw, and cheese; choose one that offers the most grating and slicing options.

Scales, measuring jugs and metric cups and spoons

There are times when ingredients must be carefully weighed or measured and nothing is more precise than a set of electronic scales. In this book, a graduated jug with a capacity of at least one litre with graduations in millilitres and metric cups is essential for liquids. A metric cup, half cup and quarter cup are handy for measuring smaller quantities of flour and sugar, or for liquids. For small quantities, the measures used in this book are standard: 1 metric tablespoon (20 ml), ½ tablespoon (10 ml) and 1 teaspoon (5 ml).

Other practical items include:

*   A large colander for draining vegetables, fruits and pasta, and a fine strainer for straining sauces and sifting flour.

*   Pastry cutters or PVC rings to help you plate food.

*   Wooden spoons, egg lifter, large spoons, skimmer, slotted spoon, ladle.

*   A pastry brush to brush pans with a small amount of oil.

*   A pepper grinder.

*   A salad spinner to dry leafy greens.

Prepare mixed salads with a
variety of fresh seasonal greens.

COOKING & EATING FOR WELL-BEING

'Our food is our medicine', 'We are what we eat'. If we believe these two sayings, then the cook has a most important role to play in our well-being. In the role of the 'cook as doctor', a role that marries gastronomy with science, a good cook prepares delicious concoctions which 'service' all functions of the body. The medicine of a good cook gives more pleasure than that of the doctor, and acts as a preventer of disease and illness rather than as a cure.

To help us become thoughtful cooks, we need the aid of science. The Anti-Cancer Council of Victoria and other health organisations have provided us with dietary guidelines with which we should all become familiar if we want to improve our cooking and eating for long-lasting health. Those dietary guidelines are spelt out here – this is not a fad diet, but a guide to encourage people to become better cooks and healthier and happier eaters.

Get into a Regular Eating Pattern

On several occasions in this book I talk about the benefits of learning from people who are older than us, who have a lifetime of experience behind them. From my grand-mother, who lived until a hundred, and from my father, I learnt about the importance of eating proper, balanced meals at a regular time each day, meals that are modified according to my lifestyle.

Eating should be a pleasurable experience from the time you begin the meal until the end of the digestion of the food. Before a meal you should have an appetite, but if you have been starving for the past hour it either means that you did not eat enough nutritious food at the previous meal, or that you left too much of a break between meals. Try to get into an eating routine so that each meal keeps you satisfied until the next. If you must have a long break between meals, try to plan for a nourishing snack, such as a sandwich, fruit or a healthy slice in-between. Above all, avoid quick fixes like fatty foods or foods high in added sugar.

My grandmother often praised the habit of eating a light dinner in order to enjoy a good night's rest. Then, on waking, you are ready for a full breakfast that will take you to your next meal, and so on. The body does not appreciate too many snacks all the time; like us, the digestive system needs to rest. You will see that the body is like a clock and one of the bonuses of a regular eating routine is regular bowel movements.

Because eating is a moment of intimacy between us and our food, we should make time to eat and try not to eat on the run. Eating is a more pleasant experience physically and healthier for the digestive system if we are comfortably seated and not standing, walking or driving. I believe that noisy situations should be avoided. Where the noise levels are low, you can better appreciate the delicate and natural flavours of food. It has also been shown that people tend to choose foods that are saltier, sweeter and higher in fat in noisy environments. Think about that and test it out the next time you eat!

Take small mouthfuls and chew the food well to enhance digestion. Drink slowly. And whenever possible, share meals with those you love.

Listen to how your body feels after eating to get an indication of your digestion. Work out which foods, if any, cause problems, such as stomach burn, bad digestion, wind and so on. Establish the meals that make you feel good and those that make you feel uncomfortable. Avoid overloading the digestive system and learn to feel when you have had enough. Over a long period of time, finding out which foods suit you and which don't will keep you healthy.

Identify Bad Eating Habits and Slowly Change Them

I have an Italian friend who drizzles at least one tablespoon of olive oil over almost every dish he sits down to; every member of my family in France used to spoon at least three teaspoons of sugar into their morning cup of coffee; many people season their food with salt before they even taste it.

These three examples illustrate some common eating habits. Whether good or bad, such habits are inherited either from our cultural background, from the way our parents fed us, from peer pressure (children, adolescents, workplace), from those we currently live with or our lifestyle. To work out our eating habits, we first need to know about the recommended dietary guidelines and pay attention to the way we feel after eating and digesting. Following are some common inappropriate eating habits that need to be addressed:

- eating too few vegetables and insufficient fibre foods (bread, cereals)

- eating too much fatty food

- eating too much meat

- drinking too much coffee and sweet soft drinks

- drinking too much alcohol

- eating too many sweet foods

- eating too much salty food

You will have more success in changing inappropriate eating habits if you do it slowly. For example, if you usually put two teaspoons of sugar in your coffee, first cut it down to one-and-a-half teaspoons, then reduce it to one teaspoon, and so on. If you drink too much coffee, start by drinking a smaller cup, then alternate a cup of coffee with a glass of water or fresh fruit juice. Substitute rich snacks with fresh fruit, or drink freshly squeezed fruit or vegetable juice.

EAT A WIDE VARIETY OF FOOD

All health bodies, including the Anti-Cancer Council, National Heart Foundation, diabetes organisations and government health departments agree that the most important guideline for a healthy diet is to eat a wide variety of foods. Those who love good food and those who cook could not hope for a better guideline, for it means that we can use all kinds of food in our cooking. Nothing is considered 'bad'; everything is 'good' in moderation. The great advantage of eating a wide range of foods is that it supplies all the nutrients needed by the various parts of the body. All foods have a role to play.

Enjoy Plenty of Vegetables

I have noticed that most people enjoy vegetables more and more as they grow older. I personally love the textures, colours and flavours of vegetables, the way they are easy to chew and digest, and especially the way they make me feel at the end of a meal. They are simply good for us and have a positive effect on our health. In terms of volume, we need to eat vegetables in the greatest quantity. Vegetables are an excellent source of vitamins, minerals and dietary fibre. They help protect us against many cancers, especially those related to the digestive system, as well as many other diseases.

The challenge for our society is to ensure that young people enjoy and understand from a young age the value of vegetables. Take carrots, for example, one of the vegetables with the most goodness. They can be eaten raw, either whole as a snack, or grated in salads and sandwiches, or cut into small sticks and eaten with dips. Carrots can be sliced or diced for a soup or casserole. They can be stir-fried, steamed or puréed. Most children would enjoy carrots in at least one of these ways. Of course, parents ought not to force children to eat something they don't want, but try to understand that it may not be the actual vegetable but the way it is cooked – and the texture – that the children dislike.

Nutritional experts particularly recommend eating generous portions of yellow vegetables, such as carrots and pumpkin, green leafy vegetables, such as spinach and salad greens, and members of the cabbage family, such as cauliflower, bok choy, broccoli, brussels sprouts and Chinese broccoli. The fibre content of vegetables helps neutralise

There are many varieties
of Chinese vegetables
available these days, and
I think they are superb.

some cancer-causing substances, reduces the time the food stays in the intestine and helps reduce the absorption of fat by the body. (Excess fat is one of the factors that favours the development of some cancers and other diseases.)

In addition, the various vitamins and other chemicals present in vegetables play an important role in reducing the development of cancer. Some vegetables are known to counteract the toxic substances formed when meat and fish are burnt or overcooked.

Enjoy Several Serves of Cereals Daily

Cereals hold pride of place in all ancient societies, and the word 'cereal' itself takes its name from Ceres, the Roman goddess of agriculture. Cereals are a good source of complex carbohydrates, which provide long-lasting energy. Rice is the most popular cereal of all and remains an everyday food for over half the world's population. My Chinese friends claim to feel unwell if they don't eat rice for a few days, and some Italians are lost if deprived of their beloved pasta. Personally, I feel a bit unwell if I don't eat bread. Apart from rice, the other major cereals are wheat, oats, corn and barley. We should take every opportunity to consume some form of cereal daily. Having it for breakfast is an excellent way to start the day, and it is preferable that it does not contain extras like fats, sugar or chocolate. Enjoy mixed cereals with low-fat milk or soy milk. If a meal lacks cereal in the form of either pasta, couscous, or rice, substitute with a nourishing wholemeal or wholegrain bread.

Alternate Moderate Serves of Meat, Fish and Vegetarian Protein

For those who routinely eat large quantities of fatty meat, try alternating with moderate serves of other lean meat, fish, dairy products, eggs, vegetarian protein and vegetables. Fatty diets are incompatible with long-lasting good health. Most of us would benefit from eating fish two or three times a week, but avoid deep-fried fish and fish served with fatty or creamy sauces. Depending on your appetite, a moderate portion of fish is between 125–200 g (4–7 oz).

Trim away all visible fat from meat and remove the skin from chicken before cooking. Limit portions of lean meat to about 125–150 g (4–5 oz) per person.

Pulses such as dried beans, lentils and chickpeas are a superb source of low-fat protein and we would do well to eat them more often. It is best, however, to avoid eating a large quantity of pulses at one sitting as this may be hard on the digestion. A moderate serve of cooked pulses is between ¾ cup and 1 cup. Pulses are best eaten with cereal foods, such as bread, pasta or rice as these foods complement one another.

It is good to eat nuts regularly but in very small quantities as they have a high fat content.

Eggs and dairy products are another source of protein that can be enjoyed in moderation as part of a varied diet.

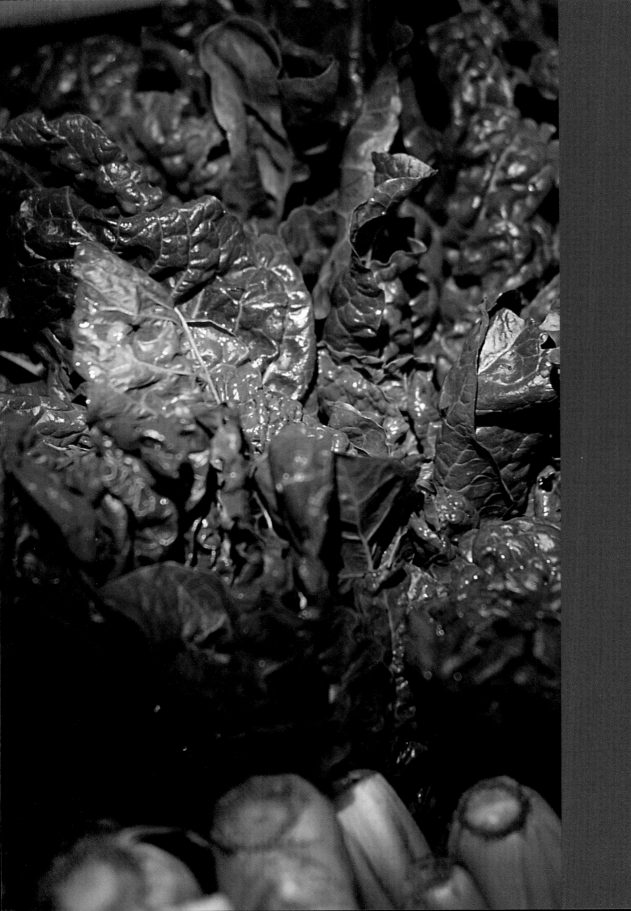

Eat Several Serves of Fruit Daily

I was lucky growing up as a child in France: we had lots of fruit trees around our house so there was always fresh fruit all year round. We had pears, apples and various other fruits, and, being French, we often ate bread with fruit as a snack. Our modern society has unfortunately fallen into the habit of snacking on rich, processed foods that are high in sugar, fat and additives.

Fruit is a versatile food: it has wonderful flavour, great texture, needs no cooking and is so good for us. Always keep a well-stocked fruit bowl both at home and at work, and, most importantly, introduce your children to the pleasures of eating fruit with breakfast, lunch and dinner. Like vegetables, fruit is a great source of vitamins, fibre and other good things.

Consume Fatty Foods in Moderation

In 1996, half of American and Australian men are overweight. In fact, the average male's weight has increased by several kilos in the last decade.

Fat is the most energy-dense food, so if we consume more than we need, the extra energy will be stored as fat, resulting in weight gain. It is sometimes very difficult to know the fat content of some foods such as pastries, stir-fried dishes, deep-fried foods, cakes and chocolate bars. But we can learn to identify foods rich in fat by focusing on their taste and texture. If you feel you are consuming too much fat, try to cut down and ask for information about the food you eat at restaurants and take-aways.

Use a minimum of oil when cooking at home. Avoid deep-frying and use only a light coating of oil when pan-frying. Use a non-stick pan or wok when stir-frying: 1 tablespoon of oil is sufficient when stir-frying for two. All oils contain the same amount of calories. I use olive, peanut or canola oil, depending on what I am cooking, and butter for special occasions. Margarine is recommended as a substitute by the National Heart Foundation for those with a high cholesterol level. Basically, it is wise to consume butter, cream, cheese, other dairy products and margarine in moderation. Consider using low-fat dairy products and keep cream for special treats. Spread butter thinly on bread and try alternatives such as avocado, hummus, tahini and savoury nut spreads such as almond and hazelnut spread.

Salty and Spicy Foods

The family cook or cooks influences the way all members of the household eat. If we are regularly served salty food, we necessarily develop a taste for salt. In the long term excess salt can contribute to high blood pressure. Salt creates thirst and therefore discomfort, and excess salt only distracts the eater from the more subtle flavours of the food. Learn to cook using a minimum of salt and replace it with other seasonings such as herbs, spices and lemon juice. Avoid adding salt at the table before tasting the food, and read food labels carefully to ascertain salt content. Look out for hidden salt in cured and preserved foods. Some sauces such as soy sauce, fish sauce and tomato sauce can be very salty, so take time to choose carefully when eating out. We are advised by the Anti-Cancer Council to consume smoked foods in moderation, as the smoking process creates substances which can be carcinogenic. Hot, spicy foods can increase the risk of problems in the digestive system when eaten in excess.

Moderate Sugar Consumption

The increasing prevalence of fast food – the gradual Americanisation of the food we eat and drink – has had an impact on our overall sugar consumption. Refined sugar is a high source of calories and contains no nutrients other than carbohydrates. It is also a major cause of dental decay. Foods such as cakes, biscuits, desserts and chocolate bars contain a lot of sugar and fat. Go for fruits and low-fat savoury foods instead and limit these foods to occasional treats. Sugar in savoury foods also masks their natural flavours, so keep a check on its use.

Limit the consumption of sugar in coffee and tea. Choose cold drinks such as fresh fruit juices or water in preference to soft drinks with a high sugar content.

What to Drink and When

Water is the drink best suited to the human body, and an average person needs to consume 2.5 litres of water a day. Ideally, half of that amount comes from the food we eat, especially in a balanced diet that includes plenty of plant food. The rest can come from plain, unflavoured water.

Fresh fruit juices are a good source of flavour, vitamins and water. When you are out shopping or working, try one of those juices available at some take-away outlets. Fresh fruit juice first thing in the morning is a particularly good way to start the day.

If your diet is not high in fat, plain milk is good in moderation. Otherwise, try skim milk or fat-reduced, protein-enriched milk. I tend to avoid milk when I have a cold as it seems to aggravate sinus congestion. Beware of flavoured milk drinks and milk shakes that have added sugar.

It seems that a new soft drink is created every month these days. However, these cordials, processed fruit drinks and colas are high in sugar. They should be avoided, not only before meals because they cut the appetite for good food, but also in the evenings after dinner. I believe young children are better off without these drinks.

An intake of one or two standard alcoholic drinks per day such as two glasses of wine or beer is considered to be compatible with good health. If you are drinking alcohol, combine it with food to reduce the effects of alcohol on the body's metabolism. Avoid drinking on an empty stomach or between your last meal and bed time.

Excessive consumption of alcohol has been linked with many modern diseases, including cancer and liver disease. Alcohol is calorie-dense and contributes to diseases associated with obesity and malnutrition. If you know you drink too much alcohol, consider reducing your consumption slowly over time. Beer drinkers are encouraged to drink low-alcohol beer. If necessary, ask your doctor for help.

Coffee comes in different strengths and is a strong stimulant. It is best drunk in moderation. Refrain from drinking coffee on an empty stomach or in the evening after dinner. If you feel you are drinking too much coffee, alternate it with water, freshly squeezed juices or caffeine-free herbal teas. Like coffee, tea is a stimulant but not quite as strong. Drink tea in moderation and avoid it in the evening.

EATING OUT & TAKE-AWAYS

Studies have shown that we are eating out more often and that our average weight is increasing. I believe that the two are related. Eating out in a restaurant or taking food away not only provides great pleasure for all, but also gives the cook a break and is a good source of inspiration – it is always nice to see how other cooks combine, season and present food.

All restaurants and take-aways try to please their customers in one way or another, in the hope of repeat custom. Unfortunately, restaurant and take-away food is almost always higher in fat, added sugar and salt than home-cooked food, and the choice of vegetables is too limited.

The restaurant industry needs to pay attention to this and, as consumers, we would benefit from making careful choices and demands when faced with a restaurant or take-away menu. While planning your meal, try to recall when you last ate and what you ate. If, for example, you are out for breakfast and your last meal was a rich dinner with wine, then avoid eating a rich breakfast and go for light, high-energy foods such as cereal, bread and fresh fruit.

When eating out, enquire about dishes that are low in fat – but beware, you may not always receive the truth. Ask about the size of the meal and what vegetables are served with it and in what quantity. Have a look around to see the size of the serves and read the menu carefully to find a dish that is delicious and nourishing. Learn to negotiate with the restaurant waiter or the person behind the counter at the take-away shop about adapting dishes to your needs. For example, I often ask for less meat and more vegetables and for salad dressings to be served separately. It is alright to ask for smaller serves.

Watch for foods that have a high fat content such as: deep-fried foods of all kinds; dishes with a fair amount of cheese, including sauces; white sauces and butter and cream sauces; crumbed foods; chicken cooked with the skin on and meat that has not been trimmed of fat; some stir-fry dishes; smallgoods; some dressings, including mayonnaise; food wrapped in pastry; pastries, biscuits and cakes; ice-cream and chocolate.

Watch the salt content as well: foods topped with lots of cheese; pickles, anchovies, cured foods and smallgoods; dishes containing soy sauce, oyster sauce or fish sauce; food that is often automatically sprinkled with salt such as French fries and fried food.

Avoid eating several dishes containing meat protein in the one day. Choose dishes with plenty of vegetables and be very selective in the snacks you eat. When buying ready-made meals at the supermarket, read the ingredients carefully. Keep three-course meals for very special occasions.

You can be healthy and still eat a variety of foods. Take your time when you eat and learn to stop eating and drinking as soon as you feel you have had enough.

My 14 Tips for Cooking and Eating for Pleasure

1. Shop for fresh food at least three times a week and cook food at its freshest.

2. Develop a friendly relationship with fresh food people.

3. Stimulate your senses by looking at, touching, smelling and tasting new foods.

4. Take notes, write down recipes and share your cooking knowledge with those around you.

5. Eat a wide variety of foods and learn to cook new dishes regularly.

6. Enjoy plenty of vegetables, fruit and high-fibre foods like cereals.

7. Cook using a minimum of fat and consume fat and fatty foods in moderation.

8. Alternate meat, fish and vegetarian protein dishes.

9. Limit salty, smoked, sweet and hot spicy foods.

10. Drink alcohol, coffee and sweetened soft drinks in moderation.

11. Sit to eat and eat slowly.

12. Notice the content, taste, texture and effect of what you eat.

13. Watch your weight.

14. Learn to relax, exercise daily and enjoy life.

Soups are handy for the busy cook because they last for a few days and can be reheated as required. New cooks will be encouraged by the ease of preparing a simple soup. Plain single-vegetable soups such as carrot, pumpkin or broccoli, cooked with a little onion and water or stock, blended to a purée and seasoned with chopped parsley, chives or spices are really little trouble at all. A mixed vegetable soup where the vegetables are cut into small pieces and cooked together is also ideal if you want to use up the leftover bits and pieces in the fridge. Choose vegetables with contrasting flavours and texture, and either blend the cooked soup or leave it as it is. Adding potato, cooked beans, rice or small pasta transforms a soup into a light meal.

In this chapter you will find a few soup recipes containing meat or fish which can be served as a main meal. Whatever soup you make, serve it with good, fresh bread.

Asparagus Soup

Asparagus is a delicate vegetable,
so to retain all the flavour and goodness,
be careful not to overcook it.

SERVES 4

1 kg (about 2 lb) asparagus

1 teaspoon vegetable oil, such
as peanut or canola oil

¼ brown onion, finely chopped

¼ teaspoon curry powder

1 small potato, very thinly sliced

4 cups water *or* chicken stock (p. 204)

salt and freshly ground black pepper

1 teaspoon butter (optional)

2 tablespoons chopped parsley

Peel the asparagus spears with a potato peeler if they are large, starting from just below the tip and descending to the base. Snap off the hard part at the base and discard. Wash the asparagus in cold water and cut into 2.5 cm (1 in) pieces.

Heat the oil in a saucepan and, on low heat, fry the onion for 2 minutes. Add the curry powder and stir well. Add the asparagus, potato and stock or water. Bring to the boil, season with a little salt and pepper, and cook for 10–15 minutes until the vegetables are just cooked.

Blend or purée the soup and pass through a fine strainer. Just before serving, stir in the butter and the chopped parsley.

Broccoli soup with a hint of curry

You can use all parts of the broccoli
when making this soup. I enjoy this lovely
vegetable soup with bread.

SERVES 4

½ tablespoon peanut oil

1 small leek, finely sliced

1 teaspoon curry powder

5 cups chicken (p. 204) *or* vegetable
stock (p. 203)

100 g (3½ oz) pumpkin, peeled
and cut into small pieces

1 kg (about 2 lb) broccoli, cut
into small florets

salt and freshly ground black pepper

¼ cup chopped parsley

1 clove garlic, finely chopped (optional)

Heat the oil in a non-stick saucepan and stir-fry the leek and curry powder for about 3 minutes.

Add the stock and pumpkin and bring to a simmer. Add the broccoli, return to a simmer, and season with salt and pepper. Cook, uncovered, until the vegetables are soft.

Blend to a purée or pass through a food mill. Reheat the soup in a pan without boiling. Season with parsley and garlic before serving.

Pumpkin Soup with parsley & chives

You can make this soup with any type of pumpkin. Try substituting the cayenne pepper with spices like cummin or paprika – I think they are lovely variations.

SERVES 4

½ tablespoon olive oil

½ brown onion, peeled and chopped

1 kg (about 2 lb) pumpkin flesh, peeled and cut into small pieces

1 small potato, peeled and sliced

5 cups water *or* chicken stock (p. 204)

salt and freshly ground black pepper

½ cup chopped parsley

a pinch of cayenne pepper

2 tablespoons finely snipped chives

Heat the oil in a saucepan and fry the onion for a few minutes. Add the pumpkin pieces, potato and chicken stock.

Bring to a simmer, season with salt and pepper and cook uncovered until the pumpkin is soft. This usually takes about 15 minutes.

Mash or blend the soup to a purée or pass it through a food mill. Reheat the soup in pan without boiling. Stir in the parsley and cayenne pepper and serve sprinkled with chives.

Leek & carrot soup

This lovely winter soup can be served as a light evening meal with bread if you've had a big lunch. You can make this soup using other vegetables such as broccoli or cauliflower.

SERVES 4–6

2 small leeks, white part only

½ tablespoon peanut *or* canola oil

2 medium carrots, finely sliced

6 cups water *or* chicken stock (p. 204)

salt and freshly ground black pepper

2 tablespoons chopped parsley

1 clove garlic, finely chopped

Cut the leeks in four lengthwise, leaving the root end intact to keep it in one piece while washing. Wash the leek thoroughly in lukewarm water to remove any grit. Slice finely.

Heat the oil in a large non-stick saucepan and on low heat gently fry the leeks for about 4 minutes, stirring constantly. Stir in the carrots, add the stock or water, and stir well. Season with salt and pepper.

Bring to the boil and cook for about 15 minutes. Blend or mash the soup to a purée or pass it through a food mill. Stir in the parsley and garlic just before serving.

Mixed vegetable soup

The liquid of this hearty soup makes a good vegetable stock. For a light dinner, sprinkle the soup with a little freshly grated parmesan and serve it with bread.

SERVES 4

1 tablespoon peanut or canola oil

1 leek, sliced

1 carrot, finely sliced

1 stick celery, finely sliced

1/2 small swede, finely sliced

1/4 small cabbage, shredded

1/2 red or yellow capsicum, diced

salt and freshly ground black pepper

1 clove garlic, finely chopped (optional)

2 tablespoons chopped parsley

Heat the oil in a non-stick saucepan and on low heat cook the leek, carrot and celery for 3 minutes. Add the swede, cabbage and capsicum. Cover with cold water, season with a little salt and pepper and bring to a simmer. Cook for 20 minutes, uncovered.

Just before serving, stir in the garlic and parsley.

Lentil & Pumpkin Soup

This vegetarian soup is very satisfying when eaten with bread. If using dried lentils, soak them for 1 hour in cold water before cooking.

SERVES 4

1/2 tablespoon olive oil

1/2 brown onion, peeled and chopped

1/4 teaspoon curry powder

4 baby carrots, peeled and finely sliced

4 cups water

100 g (3 1/2 oz) pumpkin, peeled and diced

400 g (14 oz) can lentils, drained

salt and freshly ground black pepper

2 tablespoons chopped parsley

1 clove garlic, finely chopped

4 spring onions, finely sliced

Heat the oil in a large saucepan and on low heat stir in the onion, curry powder and carrots. Stir for about 2 minutes until the onions take on colour.

Add the water, pumpkin and drained lentils, bring to a simmer and cook until the vegetables are soft (about 15 minutes). Season with salt and pepper.

Blend half the soup to a purée. Return the purée to the pan and reheat without boiling. Stir in the parsley and garlic, and serve sprinkled with spring onions.

Mediterranean Dressing

The flavours of basil, olive oil and garlic are superb with bitter salad leaves such as curly endive and radicchio.

TO DRESS A SALAD FOR 2

½ clove garlic, finely chopped

juice of ½ lemon *or* 1 teaspoon red-wine vinegar

salt and freshly ground black pepper

1 tablespoon olive oil

4 basil leaves, finely sliced

In a bowl whisk the garlic with lemon juice and a little salt and pepper. Whisk in the olive oil and the basil.

Low-fat cream cheese & yoghurt Dressing

This dressing is a good substitute for cream or butter, and is great with baked potatoes or steamed vegetables. Look for smooth low-fat cream cheese with a fat content of less than 8 per cent. Manufacturers call it smooth creamed cottage cheese, quark or fromage blanc.

TO DRESS A SALAD FOR 2–3

1½ tablespoons low-fat skim-milk yoghurt

2½ tablespoons low-fat smooth creamed cottage cheese

1 tablespoon low-fat milk

freshly ground black pepper

2 pinches of cayenne pepper

juice of ½ lemon

1 tablespoon snipped chives *or* finely chopped parsley *or* basil

Whisk all the ingredients together until smooth. Refrigerate if you are not using it immediately.

Tahini Dressing

Tahini is a flavoursome paste made from sesame seeds. It is available in jars at most supermarkets and health-food stores.

TO DRESS A SALAD FOR 2

½ tablespoon tahini

1 tablespoon water

juice of ½ lemon

salt and freshly ground black pepper

½ small clove garlic, finely chopped

Mix the tahini with water and lemon juice. Just before serving, season with salt, pepper and chopped garlic. If you wish to make the dressing thinner, add a little extra water.

Green Salad with Walnut Dressing

The secret of a good green salad is to include different varieties of green leaves. I like to add a few nuts to give the salad a little crunch. The dressing should be flavoursome. You can, of course, add other ingredients such as tomato or avocado.

SERVES 2

2 handfuls of mixed green leaves of your choice

½ clove garlic, finely chopped (optional)

juice of ½ lemon *or* 1 teaspoon red-wine vinegar

a small pinch of curry powder

salt and freshly ground black pepper

1 tablespoon olive oil

1 tablespoon walnuts, finely chopped

1 tablespoon finely snipped chives (optional)

Gently wash the salad leaves in a large amount of cold water. Drain and dry well using a salad spinner.

In a salad bowl, thoroughly combine the garlic, lemon juice, curry powder, a little salt, pepper and oil. Add the walnuts and green leaves.

Just before serving, toss gently and sprinkle with chives.

Potato Salad

This salad is ideal for a barbecue.
I use a dill and yoghurt dressing here,
but you can use your favourite dressing.

SERVES 2

6 small potatoes

salt and freshly ground black pepper

1 teaspoon Dijon mustard

½ teaspoon red-wine vinegar

½ tablespoon natural yoghurt

½ teaspoon low-fat sour cream

1 tablespoon finely sliced dill

1 tablespoon chopped parsley

Place the washed potatoes in a small saucepan. Cover with cold water and season with a little salt. Bring to the boil and cook for about 15 minutes or until tender. Leave under cold running water until the potatoes have cooled. When almost cold, peel the potatoes and dice or cut into slices.

In a salad bowl, combine the mustard, vinegar, yoghurt and sour cream. Season with salt and pepper and mix in the dill and parsley. Toss in the potatoes and serve.

Coleslaw with a Yoghurt Dressing

Using yoghurt instead of mayonnaise
makes this coleslaw a very healthy preparation.
This dish is excellent for barbecues.

SERVES 4

2 pinches of curry powder

juice of 1 lemon

3 tablespoons natural yoghurt

freshly ground black pepper

½ small white onion, finely chopped

1 tablespoon sultanas

1 tablespoon chopped cashew nuts

¼ fresh, green cabbage, finely shredded or grated

1 medium carrot, peeled and grated

2 spring onions, finely sliced

To make the dressing, mix the curry powder, lemon juice, yoghurt, black pepper, white onion, sultanas and cashew nuts in a salad bowl.

Toss in the cabbage and carrot, sprinkle with the sliced spring onions and serve.

Bean & Artichoke Salad with sun-dried tomato dressing

This popular salad is ideal for a barbecue.

SERVES 4

300 g (11 oz) young green beans

4 basil leaves, finely sliced

2 sun-dried tomatoes, finely sliced

juice of ½ lemon

1 tablespoon olive oil

1 clove garlic, finely chopped

freshly ground black pepper

8 canned or bottled artichoke hearts, drained

2 tomatoes, quartered

Bring a large saucepan of salted cold water to the boil. Drop in the beans and cook until they are tender. Drain and dip the beans in icy-cold water to stop the cooking process. Drain again.

Place the basil and sun-dried tomatoes in a salad bowl. Stir in the lemon juice, olive oil, garlic and pepper. Add the artichoke hearts, beans and tomatoes to the bowl. Toss gently to distribute the flavours, and serve.

Sprouts & Snowpea Salad

Toss this salad in an Asian-style dressing. I like to use mung sprouts, but use the variety you prefer.

SERVES 2

100 g (3½ oz) bean sprouts

150 g (5 oz) snowpeas, topped and tailed

juice of ½ lemon

¼ teaspoon sesame oil

1 teaspoon peanut or canola oil

½ tablespoon low-salt soy sauce

½ clove garlic, finely chopped

¼ red chilli, finely sliced (optional)

freshly ground black pepper

1 tablespoon sesame seeds

1 tablespoon finely snipped chives or coriander

Wash the sprouts and discard any blemished ones.

Place the snowpeas in a bowl and cover with boiling water. Drain after 2 minutes and refresh in cold water. Drain again.

In a small bowl mix the lemon juice with the sesame oil, peanut oil, soy sauce, garlic, chilli and pepper. Season the sprouts with half of this dressing and the snowpeas with the remaining dressing.

Place the drained snowpeas in the centre of a plate. Place the sprouts around the snowpeas, sprinkle with sesame seeds and chives or coriander, and serve.

Beetroot & Bean Salad with parsley dressing

Use your favourite beans (borlotti, cannellini) for this salad. It is full of flavour and interesting textures. This dish is also ideal for vegetarians.

SERVES 3–4

2 tablespoons low-fat natural yoghurt

2 teaspoons red-wine vinegar

2 tablespoons chopped parsley

freshly ground black pepper

400 g (14 oz) can beans

2 or 3 beetroots, cooked, peeled and diced

2 spring onions, finely sliced

To make the dressing, combine the yoghurt, vinegar and parsley in a bowl. Season generously with black pepper.

Drain the beans and rinse them briefly. Add the beans and beetroot to the dressing and mix well to incorporate. Sprinkle with spring onions before serving. If you are not serving immediately, refrigerate the salad and take out 10 minutes before serving.

Waldorf Salad

The traditional Waldorf salad contains mayonnaise and cream. My offering successfully replaces them with a yoghurt dressing. The result is a light and delicious salad.

SERVES 3–4

1 tablespoon sultanas

2 tablespoons natural yoghurt

2 sticks celery, preferably from the centre, sliced

2 Jonathan or other apples, diced

1/2 cup walnut flesh

freshly ground black pepper

juice of 1/2 lemon

a few leaves from a butter lettuce

Mix the sultanas with the yoghurt in a bowl. Add the celery and apple and stir well. Add the walnuts, pepper and lemon juice and stir again.

Line a salad bowl with the washed and dried lettuce leaves. Spoon over the salad and serve.

Every French family would have a version of this popular summer dish.

Salade Niçoise

This is my version of a famous salad that originated in
Nice, a French town on the Riviera near the Italian border.
More than a salad, it is a light meal full of flavour and texture.

SERVES 6

2 medium potatoes

2 eggs

200 g (7 oz) young French beans

2 teaspoons red-wine vinegar

1 teaspoon Dijon mustard (optional)

salt and freshly ground black pepper

2 tablespoons olive oil

6–12 butter lettuce leaves, from
the heart

2 tomatoes, sliced or cut into sixths or
about 18 cherry tomatoes, halved

3 canned or bottled artichoke hearts,
quartered

1 small brown or red onion,
peeled and thinly sliced

200 g (7 oz) can tuna in oil

24 black olives, pitted

6 anchovy fillets, cut in half lengthwise

Wash the potatoes and place in a saucepan. Cover with cold water, add a little salt and bring to the boil. Cook for about 25 minutes until the potatoes are soft. Remove from the pan and allow to cool in cold water. Peel and slice.

Place the eggs in a saucepan, cover with cold water and bring to the boil. Cover the pan, switch off the heat and leave the eggs for 14 minutes. Remove the eggs from the pan and place in a bowl of cold water to cool. Peel and slice.

Top and tail the beans and add to a medium saucepan of boiling water. Cook for 4–8 minutes until the beans are tender. Drain and place in a bowl of icy water to cool. Drain again.

Thoroughly combine the vinegar, mustard and a little salt and pepper. Mix in the olive oil.

Line a salad bowl with the washed lettuce leaves. Add the tomatoes, artichokes, onions, potatoes and beans. Pour over the dressing and top with the eggs, tuna, olives and anchovies.

Alternatively serve the salad in individual plates as shown in the photograph opposite.

Tunisian Tuna & Egg Salad ·

This refreshing salad was inspired by a trip to Tunisia a couple of years ago.
The dish can be a light meal eaten with bread or an entrée for a warm-weather lunch.
For this recipe I use a North African chilli paste called harissa, available from gourmet
delis and some supermarkets. Use an Asian-style chilli paste if you can't find it.

SERVES 6–8

2 teaspoons red-wine vinegar
  or juice of 1 lemon

2 tablespoons olive oil

3 mint leaves, finely sliced

½ teaspoon harissa *or* Asian-style
  chilli paste (optional)

1 red or green capsicum, seeded
  and diced

½ small globe fennel *or*
  ½ cucumber, diced

½ brown *or* red onion, diced

3 tomatoes, diced

salt and freshly ground black pepper

200 g (7 oz) can tuna in oil

2 hard-boiled eggs, sliced

1 tablespoon small capers

a few black olives

To make the dressing, combine the vinegar, olive oil, mint and harissa in a large bowl.

Toss the capsicum, fennel, onion and tomato with the dressing and season to taste with salt and pepper.

Spoon the salad onto plates or a serving dish. Top with the flaked tuna, egg, capers and olives, and serve.

Thai-style cabbage & bean sprout salad

It's worth learning to make this salad for the dressing alone.
You may wish to serve a grilled fish with it.

SERVES ABOUT 4

¼ Chinese cabbage, finely shredded

a handful of bean sprouts

10 cm (4 in) lemongrass stalk,
    white part only, finely chopped

juice of 2 limes *or* 1 lemon

1 tablespoon fish sauce

1 red chilli, seeded and finely sliced

1 clove garlic, chopped

1 teaspoon peanut oil

2 tablespoons coriander leaves

Bring a large saucepan of water to the boil. Cook the cabbage for 2 minutes in boiling water then drain. Refresh in cold water for a few minutes and drain again.

Wash and remove any damaged bean sprouts.

In a large bowl combine the lemongrass, lime or lemon juice, fish sauce, chilli, garlic and oil. Toss the drained cabbage and bean sprouts in the dressing and sprinkle with coriander leaves.

LIGHT M

snacks

Whether having a snack at home or outside, the best choice is one that will complement the other meals of the day. Choose snacks that are high in long-lasting energy but low in fat and sugar. The favourite snack of the Chinese is a bowl of rice or noodles with a few vegetables or meat or some broth, while Europeans tend to go for something savoury on bread. Chocolate bars and fried foods are not ideal snacks and parents need to influence their children into making good food choices from a young age. Excellent savoury snacks include salad sandwiches, soups, low-fat dairy products, low-fat noodle, pasta and rice dishes and low-fat, low-sugar breakfast cereals. If you need something sweet, have a freshly squeezed fruit juice, some fresh fruit or a slice of cake that has a low-fat, low-sugar content.

Avocado & salad on Rye

A little avocado in a sandwich gives richness and smoothness and replaces butter or margarine in a satisfying way.

SERVES 1

2 large slices rye bread

¼ avocado

½ medium carrot, grated

½ tomato, sliced

a little alfalfa *or* shredded lettuce

salt and freshly ground black
    pepper (optional)

Place the bread on a chopping board and spread with avocado.

Top one slice with carrot, tomato and alfalfa. Season with salt and pepper, close the sandwich and cut in half.

Curried egg sandwich

This sandwich makes an ideal (and quick) lunch.

SERVES 1

1 egg

1 teaspoon olive oil or butter

a pinch of curry powder, or to taste

salt and freshly ground black pepper

2 slices wholemeal, wholegrain or rye bread

3 thin slices tomato

3 tablespoons finely shredded lettuce

Place the egg in a small saucepan. Cover with cold water and bring to the boil. Cover the pan, turn off the heat and leave for 14 minutes.

Remove the egg from the water. Shell and cool a little, if necessary. Mash the egg on a plate using a fork, then incorporate the oil or butter. Season to taste with the curry powder and a little salt and pepper.

Spread the egg on both slices of bread. Top one slice with the tomato and lettuce. Top with other slice of bread and cut the sandwich in half. *Bon appetit!*

chef's note

Wrap the sandwich in foil or plastic film if not eating within 15 minutes and refrigerate on a very hot day.

Tuna & salad sandwich

This sandwich is especially good on rye bread.
Use your favourite canned tuna in olive oil.

SERVES 1

2 tablespoons canned tuna in oil, drained

3 tablespoons grated carrot

3 tablespoons shredded lettuce

freshly ground black pepper

2 slices rye bread

Break the tuna into small pieces and mix gently
in a bowl with the carrot and lettuce. Season with
a little pepper.

Spoon the tuna and salad onto one slice of bread.
Top with the second slice, cut the sandwich in half
and serve.

Beef burger & salad in a roll

You can also use chicken for this dish. If you
wish, season the meat with herbs and spices.

SERVES 1

a sprig of parsley, finely chopped

1 tablespoon cold water

125 g (¼ lb) lean ground beef

salt and freshly ground black pepper

a little oil

1 wholemeal roll

¼ avocado

2 tablespoons finely shredded lettuce

1 teaspoon mayonnaise (optional)

3 thin slices tomato

In a bowl and using your hands, thoroughly mix
the parsley, water, mince and pepper. Form into
a burger shape of about 2 cm (¾ in) thickness.

Brush a small non-stick frying pan with oil. Heat
the pan and cook the burger on medium heat.
Avoid pushing or moving the meat as it cooks.
Cook for 3 to 5 minutes on each side, depending
on how you like your meat, turning the burger
halfway through. Season with a little salt if you
wish.

Meanwhile, cut the roll in half and spread the
avocado on each side. To the base of the roll add
the shredded lettuce, then top with the burger,
mayonnaise and tomato slices. Pop the top on the
roll and serve.

Quick Pizza on Pita

This popular snack is ready in 15 minutes. You can create your own toppings, using finely sliced vegetables of your choice. Use cheese moderately.

SERVES 1

1 small slice pita bread

1 tablespoon grated low-fat cheese

1 small tomato, finely sliced

salt and freshly ground black pepper

2 mushrooms, finely sliced

1 teaspoon olive oil

Preheat the oven to 220°C (450°F).

Place the pita bread on an oven tray. Sprinkle a third of the cheese over and top with slices of tomato, overlapping slightly as you go. Season with a little salt and pepper and top with the mushrooms and the remaining cheese. Drizzle the olive oil over the top and bake in a preheated oven for about 10 minutes.

Nachos

Teenagers love nachos as a snack. The dish is often prepared using a Mexican-style tomato salsa available from supermarkets, but I have provided a simple recipe for a delicious salsa.

SERVES 2

$1/4$ teaspoon chilli paste

$1/4$ teaspoon ground cummin

1 teaspoon red-wine vinegar

1 teaspoon olive oil

1 large tomato, diced

$1 1/2$ cups Italian-style tomato sauce, bottled or home-made (p. 210)

2 spring onions, finely sliced (optional)

about 150 g (5 oz) plain corn chips

about 100 g ($3 1/2$ oz) grated low-fat mozzarella

Preheat the oven to 180°C (350°F).

To make the salsa, in a small bowl mix together the chilli paste, cummin, vinegar and olive oil. Add the diced tomato, tomato sauce and spring onions, and mix well.

Place the corn chips in a shallow ovenproof dish. Sprinkle with a third of the cheese. Top with the salsa and remaining cheese. Bake in the preheated oven for about 10 minutes or until the cheese has melted. Serve immediately.

Plain pizza dough

Making a pizza dough is like making bread dough. It is easier and
quicker when done in an electric mixer but try mixing it by hand once to develop
a 'feel' for the dough. Gluten flour is readily available from supermarkets.

MAKES 2 LARGE PIZZA BASES OR 2 LARGE FOCACCIA

2 cups lukewarm water, made with ¾ cup
boiling water and 1¼ cups cold water

2 teaspoons sugar

2 x 7 g sachets dry yeast

3¼ cups unbleached white flour, sifted

5 tablespoons gluten flour

1 teaspoon salt

2 tablespoons olive oil

Pour a quarter of the lukewarm water into a bowl and
add a pinch of sugar. Whisk in the yeast until dissolved.
Leave for about 5 minutes until the mixture starts to
bubble.

Sift the flours into a large mixing bowl. Add the salt and
remaining sugar, and make a well in the centre.

Add the remaining water and oil to the yeast mixture
and pour this into the well in the centre of the flour.
Incorporate the liquid into the flour either by hand or
with an electric mixer until it forms a thick sticky paste.
Mix well for about 2 minutes. Add a little extra flour if
the mixture is too runny, or a little water if it's too dry.
Cover the bowl with a clean tea towel and leave to rise
in a warm place for about 1 hour or until the dough has
doubled in bulk.

Flour the workbench and your hands and tip out the
dough onto the bench. Punch down. Divide the dough
into two or more pieces, depending on whether you are
making a small or large pizza. Shape the piece of
dough into a ball.

Rest the dough for about 10 minutes before rolling out
to make your pizza or focaccia.

Mushroom & olive Roll

This savoury roll is superb as a light meal served with a salad. The secret of the dish is to mix and roll the scone-like dough rapidly and to cook it without delay.

SERVES 6–8

1 teaspoon olive oil

400 g (14 oz) mushrooms of your choice, sliced

1 tablespoon tomato paste

1 clove garlic, finely chopped

6 spring onions, finely diced

2 tablespoons finely sliced basil

½ cup grated mozzarella

12 black olives, pitted and finely sliced

a pinch of salt

2 cups self-raising flour

30 g (1 oz) butter

about ¾ cup milk

1 egg, lightly beaten for glazing

Heat the oil in a large non-stick frying pan and cook the mushrooms until soft. Place the mushrooms in a bowl to cool. Mix the tomato paste, garlic, spring onions, basil, cheese and olives into the cooled mushrooms and season with salt.

Preheat the oven to 200°C (400°F).

Sift the flour into a bowl and, using your fingertips, rub the butter and flour together until the mixture resembles fine breadcrumbs. Make a well in the centre and gradually stir in the milk to form a soft dough. You may need to add a little extra milk if the mixture is too dry or flour if it's too sticky.

Roll out the dough on a lightly floured surface to a 30 cm (12 in) square. Spread the mushroom preparation evenly over the dough and brush the edges with the beaten egg. Roll it up like a Swiss roll and glaze the top with the remaining egg.

Carefully transfer the roll to a greased baking tray and bake in the preheated oven for 30 minutes or until golden brown. Cut into slices and serve hot or cold.

Capsicum & herb Bread

Serve this with antipasto at a barbecue or outdoor lunch.
It can also be baked as a focaccia or pizza base. You will need a greased bread tin.

MAKES 1 LOAF

1 tablespoon olive oil

½ red capsicum, finely diced

1 tablespoon finely chopped fresh thyme

3 sun-dried tomatoes, finely sliced

12 Greek olives, pitted and finely sliced

1 teaspoon honey

½ cup chopped parsley

1¾ cups lukewarm water, made from ¾ cup boiling water and 1 cup cold water

2 x 7 g sachets dry yeast *or* 30 g (1 oz) fresh yeast

3 cups unbleached plain white flour, sifted

1 cup stoneground plain wholemeal flour

¼ teaspoon salt

Heat the oil in a non-stick saucepan and on low heat gently fry the capsicum and thyme for about 4 minutes. Transfer to a plate and allow to cool. When cool, mix in the sun-dried tomatoes, olives, honey and parsley.

In a small bowl whisk half of the lukewarm water with the yeast until dissolved.

Place both flours in a large mixing bowl with the salt. Incorporate the yeast mixture and remaining water with the flour, using either one hand or an electric mixer. When the liquid and flour are combined, mix in the cooked vegetable and herb mixture. Cover the bowl with a clean tea-towel and leave on the bench or in a warm place to rise for about 40 minutes.

Flour the workbench and your hands and tip out the dough. Knead with both hands for about 2 minutes. You will feel the dough becoming firmer and more elastic. Form the dough into a sausage shape to fit your greased tin, and place into the tin with the seam underneath. Leave to rise until the dough almost reaches the rim. This takes about 20 minutes.

Preheat the oven to 220°C (450°F).

Bake the dough in preheated oven for about 35–40 minutes. Tip out onto a cake rack and check that the bread is cooked by tapping the bottom of the loaf. It should sound hollow. If necessary, return the loaf to the oven to cook a little more. Allow to cool before storing. The loaf keeps well for 2–3 days.

Mushroom medley on capsicum toast

Several types of cultivated exotic mushrooms like shiitake, enoki and cloud ear are now available almost all year round. This dish is particularly lovely if you have access to wild mushrooms in autumn.

SERVES 6

300 g (10 oz) mushrooms, mixed varieties of your choice

2 tablespoons olive oil

1 shallot, finely chopped

1 clove garlic, finely chopped

2 tablespoons chopped parsley

salt and freshly ground black pepper

6 large slices of capsicum and herb bread, toasted (p. 71)

Rinse the mushrooms briefly and slice.

Heat the oil in a non-stick frying pan and sauté the mushrooms and shallots until the mushrooms are cooked. Stir in the garlic and parsley and season with salt and pepper.

Serve on slices of hot toast.

Focaccia with olives & thyme

Focaccia is a flat Italian bread usually seasoned with herbs, spices and vegetables. Serve this as an antipasto or a light lunch. You need a greased oven tray (or two) to hold the focaccia.

MAKES 2 LARGE FOCACCIA (8–12 SLICES)

1 quantity of plain pizza dough (p. 69)

2 tablespoons olive oil

freshly ground black pepper

1 tablespoon chopped fresh lemon thyme

2 cloves garlic, finely chopped

about 16 Greek olives, pitted and halved lengthwise

100 g (3½ oz) low-fat mozzarella, grated

Preheat the oven to 250°C (500°F).

Divide the pizza dough in half and press or roll out the two pieces of dough to a circle or oval of about 2 cm (¾ in) thickness.

In a small bowl, mix together the olive oil, pepper, thyme and garlic. Brush this mixture over the dough and press in the olive halves. Sprinkle with the cheese and bake in a preheated oven for about 10 minutes or until cooked. The base must be browned.

chef's note

Excellent focaccia toppings include sun-dried tomatoes, anchovies, onion rings and various cheeses. Avoid too many salty seasonings.

Baked eggs & tomato

This dish is good with a mixed vegetable salad. You will need 2 individual porcelain or pottery soufflé moulds. If you wish, replace the tomato with ratatouille (p. 119), the popular vegetable dish from the south of France.

SERVES 1

a little olive oil to grease the soufflé moulds

4 slices tomato, about 1 cm (⅓ in) thick *or* 4 tablespoons Italian-style tomato sauce, bottled or home-made (p. 210)

about 3 basil leaves *or* parsley *or* tarragon, finely chopped

2 medium eggs

salt and freshly ground black pepper

Grease the soufflé moulds with olive oil.

Place 2 cm (¾ in) of hot water in a small oven dish. Preheat the oven to 180°C (350°F).

Place one tomato slice or 1 tablespoon Italian tomato sauce in each soufflé mould and sprinkle with the basil. Break an egg over the top and season with a little salt and pepper. Top with the remaining tomato slices or sauce, and season with more pepper.

Stand the moulds in the hot water and bake in the oven for about 5 minutes, or a little longer if you like the yolk more cooked.

Omelette with mushrooms & Herbs

This dish can be adapted to suit your taste and what you have in the refrigerator. Use a non-stick frying pan.

SERVES 1

2 eggs

1 teaspoon vegetable oil

1 teaspoon butter *or* olive oil

½ cup sliced mushrooms

about 50 g (almost 2 oz) bean sprouts (optional)

2 spring onions, sliced

½ tablespoon sliced coriander leaves

salt and freshly ground black pepper

Beat the eggs in a bowl.

Heat the oil and butter in a non-stick frying pan and fry the mushrooms for about 3 minutes. Add the bean sprouts and stir for 20 seconds before adding the beaten eggs, spring onions, coriander leaves and a little salt and pepper. Stir the egg gently in the pan to enable it to cook quickly. Serve hot when the eggs have set.

Fried eggs with ratatouille

This is the kind of light meal I enjoy with bread when I am cooking for one.
You only need a small frying pan to prepare this.

SERVES 1

1 teaspoon olive oil

a sprig of thyme, chopped

¼ onion, peeled and diced

¼ red capsicum, diced

1 small zucchini, diced

¼ small eggplant, diced

1 tomato, diced

salt and freshly ground black pepper

a pinch of cayenne pepper

1 or 2 eggs

Heat the olive oil in a small non-stick frying pan. Add thyme and onion to the pan and stir for 1 minute. Add the capsicum, stir for a further minute then add the zucchini, eggplant and tomato. Cook until the vegetables are soft. This takes about 5–10 minutes. Season with salt, pepper and cayenne.

Make a hollow in the centre of the vegetables. Break the egg into the centre, cover the pan and cook until the white of the egg has set. Season the egg yolk with black pepper and serve immediately.

Vegetable samosas

I use ready-made filo pastry to make these delicious vegetable parcels. To make neat samosas, it is preferable to use two layers of filo at a time. You can assemble the samosas ahead of time and cook them at the last minute. You will need 2 greased baking sheets.

MAKES ABOUT 15 SAMOSAS

1 tablespoon peanut oil

¼ brown onion, chopped

1 clove garlic, chopped

1 teaspoon grated ginger

½ red capsicum, finely diced

1 tomato, finely diced

½ teaspoon curry powder

½ teaspoon turmeric

¼ teaspoon chilli paste

½ teaspoon cummin

1 medium carrot, peeled and steamed or boiled until soft

1 medium yellow sweet potato, peeled and steamed or boiled until soft

½ cup shelled peas, cooked

10 sheets filo pastry

Heat the oil in a medium saucepan and fry the onion, garlic and ginger until transparent.

Add the capsicum and tomato and cook on low heat for about 5 minutes, stirring from time to time. Add the curry powder, turmeric, chilli paste and cummin, and cook for an extra minute.

Dice the cooked carrot and sweet potato and mix with the capsicum and tomato preparation. Leave the vegetables to cool.

Brush the two baking sheets with a little oil and preheat the oven to 200°C (400°F).

Place two sheets of filo on top of each other with the narrow side towards you. Cut in three lengthwise. Place 1 tablespoon of the cold vegetables at the base of one of the long rectangles of double filo, about 2 cm (¾ in) inside the edge. Now fold the bottom right-hand corner over to meet the left-hand side of the rectangle. This forms a small triangle at the base. Continue folding the triangle over upon itself, bottom corner towards opposite side, until you reach the top. Make the rest of the samosas in the same way.

Place the samosas on oiled baking sheet and brush the top of each with a little oil. Cook in a preheated oven for 15–20 minutes until golden.

Wholemeal Bread

We enjoy this quick-and-easy bread toasted for breakfast and in sandwiches.

MAKES 1 LOAF

3 cups stoneground plain wholemeal flour

1 1/2 cups unbleached white flour

1/2 cup soy flour

2 tablespoons unprocessed bran

1/2 teaspoon salt

1 tablespoon molasses

1 tablespoon peanut or canola oil

2–2 1/4 cups warm water

30 g (about 1 oz) fresh yeast

Place the three types of flour, bran and salt in a large bowl with the molasses and oil.

Add half of the warm water to a second bowl. Crumble the yeast into the water and whisk until dissolved. Add the remaining water to the yeast mixture.

If you are using a food mixer, attach the dough hook, and mix the flour and the liquid little by little until the dough forms a ball and comes away from the side of the bowl. If you are mixing by hand, work the yeasty liquid into the ingredients in the large bowl, gradually incorporating the remaining water until the dough comes away from the side of the bowl. This takes about 1 minute. Cover with a tea-towel and leave to rise for about 30–45 minutes.

Flour your hands and the workbench to prevent the dough from sticking and remove from the bowl. Knead hard with both hands for about 2 minutes.

Form the dough into a sausage shape to fit your greased tin and place in the tin with the seam underneath. Leave to rise until the dough comes to just above the rim of the tin. This takes about 20 minutes.

Meanwhile, preheat the oven to 220°C (450°F).

Bake the bread in a preheated oven for about 35–40 minutes. When cooked, the sides of the bread are a golden brown colour and the bottom of the loaf should make a hollow sound when tapped. If necessary, return it to the oven. Tip the bread onto a cake rack to cool. The loaf keeps for 2–3 days.

chef's note

To make the bread lighter, I have used a ratio of one-third plain white flour to two-thirds wholemeal flour, but these proportions may be altered to suit your own taste.

Smoked salmon & Avocado parcels.

These parcels make a lovely special occasion entrée or light main course.
You can use a small porcelain cup measuring about 6 cm (2½ in) in diameter
to help you form the parcel.

MAKES 8 PARCELS

1 ripe tomato, diced

1 avocado, diced

1 small shallot *or* ¼ white onion,
  chopped

juice of 1 lemon

1 tablespoon finely chopped dill

salt and freshly ground black pepper

a pinch of cayenne pepper

8 large slices of smoked salmon
  or 16 smaller ones

1 tablespoon olive oil

200 g (7 oz) leafy greens

about 25 cherry tomatoes

sprigs of dill and wedges of lemon

In a medium bowl gently combine the tomato, avocado, shallots, half the lemon juice, dill, salt, pepper and cayenne pepper.

Line the inside of a small cup with a 20 cm (8 in) square piece of plastic film. Line the plastic with one large slice or two smaller slices of smoked salmon. Place half a tablespoon of the avocado preparation into the centre of the salmon and carefully fold the plastic around the salmon to form a tight parcel. Set aside and make the other parcels in the same way. Carefully peel off the plastic from the salmon. Refrigerate until required.

To make the dressing, combine the remaining lemon juice, olive oil and a little black pepper.

Place the leafy greens onto a large platter or divide into individual serving plates. Pour over the dressing. Place the salmon parcels onto the bed of greens, and garnish with the cherry tomatoes and dill. Squeeze over some lemon juice, and serve with any remaining avocado and tomato.

Fresh fruit & vegetable juice

Fruit and vegetable juices have become more popular in the past twenty years, and for good reason. Fresh juice makes an excellent drink and nourishing snack. The juice you make yourself is also much nicer than the store-bought variety, and it's so easy if you own an electric juicer.

I believe that to derive the most pleasure we should sip rather than gulp down juices. Avoid sweetening fresh fruit juice; if you must, add one teaspoon of honey for this purpose. To prepare fruit for juicing, wash the fruit well and remove any pips or stone. Peel citrus fruits and remove all the pith. It is a good idea to sprinkle a little lemon juice over delicate cut fruits such as pears and nectarines to prevent them from turning brown.

Apple & carrot juice

Apples and carrots are both full of vitamins and goodness. By juicing them you will get the most out of their nutritional value since the vitamins are more readily absorbed into the system.

SERVES 1

1 large carrot
1 large Granny Smith or other apple of
your choice

Wash the carrot and cut into small pieces to fit your juicer. Wash, quarter and core the apple. Cut into pieces.

Feed the carrot and apple pieces through the juicer and serve immediately.

Pear, Apple & Ginger Juice

This is a refreshing, spicy fruit juice, but avoid using too much ginger.

SERVES 1

1 ripe pear such as Williams
1 apple such as Granny Smith
¼ lemon
½ cm (³⁄₁₀ in) slice of ginger

Wash, quarter and core the pear and apple. Cut into pieces to fit your juicer.

Peel the lemon and ginger.

Feed the pear, apple, lemon and ginger into a juicer and drink the juice immediately.

Melon Juice:

This is a very refreshing drink, especially on a hot day. If you're unable to get all three types of melon, just replace with one of the others.

SERVES 1

100 g (3½ oz) watermelon flesh

100 g (3½ oz) rockmelon flesh

100 g (3½ oz) honeydew melon flesh

Cut or scoop out the melon flesh. Discard the pips and cut the flesh into pieces to fit your juicer. Feed through the juicer. Add a few ice-cubes to the juice, if you wish, and drink immediately.

Tomato, celery & carrot Juice

Make this delicious juice using a ripe tomato and young carrots.

SERVES 1

1 tomato

2 baby carrots

1 tender stick celery

Wash the tomato, carrots and celery and cut into small pieces. Feed through the juicer and drink immediately.

vegeta
dishes

We have such a huge variety of plant foods such as vegetables, pulses, cereals, nuts, herbs and fruits, that with just a little knowledge it is possible to create many delicious vegetarian dishes. Studies have shown that there is a lower incidence of obesity, high blood pressure, heart disease and cancers among vegetarians.

For a vegetarian dish to be a complete meal it needs to provide a combination of two types of plant food protein. Cereal grains such as wheat, oats and rice, nuts and seeds provide one type of protein, while legumes such as dried beans, lentils and chickpeas provide the rest. A dish of baked beans on wholegrain toast is a good example of a combination of the two plant food proteins.

Eggs and dairy products are an excellent source of protein. Ultimately, a vegetarian diet must be varied to provide all the nutrients the body needs. Dietary experts tell us that it is beneficial for us all to alternate meat, fish and vegetarian protein in our diet.

Hummus

Pureed beans with coriander

Hummus is a Middle-Eastern dip that is delicious served as an antipasto with raw vegetables or as a sauce for fish and grilled vegetables. It is quite readily available from gourmet food shops but it is as easy to make your own. You can use canned chickpeas or cook your own for this recipe. This dip keeps for 3 to 4 days, refrigerated.

SERVES 4–6

250 g (9 oz) cooked chickpeas

1 teaspoon ground cummin

2 pinches of salt

2 tablespoons tahini (sesame-seed paste)

juice of 1 lemon

3 tablespoons water

freshly ground black pepper

1 clove garlic, very finely chopped

Blend the chickpeas to a fine purée. Add the cummin, salt, tahini, lemon juice, water and a little pepper, then blend again. Refrigerate and, just before serving, add the chopped garlic.

This delicious purée is a practical dish for vegetarians. Try it on toast or use it as a spread for pizza or vegetarian tartlets. It can also be served simply with steamed vegetables. For this recipe, I use canned beans. The purée keeps well for 3 to 4 days in the fridge.

SERVES 2–3

400 g (14 oz) can plain beans such as cannellini or fagioli

1 tablespoon olive oil

1/4 teaspoon cummin

1/4 teaspoon chilli paste

salt and freshly ground black pepper

about 10 coriander leaves, finely sliced

In a small saucepan reheat the beans in their liquid for a few minutes. Drain and discard the liquid.

Blend the drained, cooked beans to a purée with the olive oil, cummin and chilli paste. Season. Stir in the coriander and serve.

chef's note

Unlike other foods like pasta and rice, do not season dried beans at the beginning of the cooking as salt makes them tough.

Salad of lentils, cherry tomatoes & Apple

If you have time, soak the lentils for several hours before cooking them.

SERVES 4

½ cups brown lentils

2 cummin seeds (optional)

pinch of curry powder

alt and freshly ground black pepper

teaspoon red-wine vinegar

tablespoon olive oil

50 g (9 oz) cherry tomatoes, halved or left whole

Granny Smith apple, peeled and diced

½ small white onion, chopped

tablespoons chopped parsley

oak the lentils for at least 30 minutes then drain. Place the lentils in a saucepan with the cummin eeds. Cover with three times their volume of vater and bring to the boil. Simmer for about 0 minutes or until tender. If necessary, add a little vater during cooking, but allow the liquid to vaporate towards the end. There should be very ttle liquid remaining when the lentils are cooked. Allow to cool.

o make the dressing, in a small bowl, mix ogether the curry powder, salt and a little pepper vith the vinegar. Slowly add the oil.

Place the cold lentils, cherry tomatoes and apple n a salad bowl and toss with the dressing, onion and parsley.

Home-made baked beans

I realise how much easier it is to open a can, but the beans you cook yourself are much more delicate and tasty. Choose the dried beans you like best and soak them overnight in a large quantity of cold water. When cooked, the beans keep well in the fridge for 3 to 4 days or in the freezer for 1 month.

SERVES 4

1½ cups dried beans such as cannellini, soaked overnight or for at least 12 hours

1 small brown onion, halved

2 cloves garlic, peeled and left whole

a few sprigs of parsley

½ bay leaf

a sprig of thyme

1 teaspoon tomato paste

1 cup Italian-style tomato sauce, bottled or home-made (p. 210)

salt and freshly ground black pepper

Drain the soaked beans and place in a saucepan with the onion, garlic, herbs, tomato paste and tomato sauce. Cover with water and bring to the boil.

Simmer until the beans are tender. Discard the onion, garlic and herbs and season with a little salt and pepper. Serve on your favourite toasted bread.

Vegetarian Risotto

I use a rich vegetable stock to cook this beautiful dish. If you wish, the parmesan can be replaced with 2 tablespoons of pumpkin purée or 1 tablespoon of crunchy peanut butter. Use a short, round-grain Italian rice such as Arborio for this dish.

SERVES 2

1 ½ cups vegetable stock (p. 203)

100 g (3 ½ oz) mushrooms, finely sliced

1 tablespoon olive oil

½ onion, finely chopped

½ carrot, finely chopped

10 cm (4 in) stick celery, finely chopped

½ cup risotto rice

100 g (3 ½ oz) spinach leaves, washed

1 tablespoon freshly grated parmesan

salt and freshly ground black pepper

Bring the vegetable stock and mushrooms to the boil, then reduce the heat and keep it simmering while making the risotto. Strain off the mushrooms and set aside.

Heat the oil in a medium saucepan and gently fry the chopped vegetables for about 4 minutes until soft. Add the rice and mix well for about 1 minute. Add about half a cup of stock to the rice and, while stirring, bring to a simmer. When almost all the stock has been absorbed, add another quarter cup of stock and gently stir. Keep on adding the stock, a quarter cup at a time, until the rice is cooked, but still with a firm bite in the centre. You may either have a little stock leftover or you may run out of stock, in which case use some boiling water.

Two minutes before the rice is ready, add the mushrooms and spinach. While stirring, add the parmesan and season. Taste a few grains of rice to check if it is cooked. At this point, the preparation will be creamy but not runny. Cover the risotto with a lid and allow it to rest for about 3 minutes before serving. The entire cooking process should take about 18–20 minutes.

Noodle, vegetable & spiced dried beancurd soup

This soup is the kind of meal I really love and I sometimes prepare it when on my own. The spiced dried beancurd comes in vacuum-packed plastic packs, usually containing 4 to 6 squares of beancurd. Both the beancurd and egg noodles are readily available from the refrigerated section of Chinese grocery shops and supermarkets.

SERVES 2

½ tablespoon peanut *or* canola oil

squares spiced dried beancurd, cut into matchstick-size strips

large slices ginger

stick celery, cut into long, thin strips

medium carrot, cut into long, thin strips

00 g (3½ oz) shiitake mushrooms *or* other mushrooms of your choice

cups water *or* vegetable stock (p. 203)

branches Chinese broccoli, cut diagonally into 4 cm (1¾ in) pieces

00 g (7 oz) fine Chinese egg noodles

½ tablespoon soy sauce

½ small chilli, finely sliced (optional)

0 g (2 oz) bean sprouts, washed

spring onions, finely sliced

Heat a wok and add half the oil. When the oil is hot, add the dried beancurd and stir-fry for 30 seconds. Transfer to a plate.

Heat the remaining oil and add the ginger, celery, carrot and mushrooms and stir-fry for 30 seconds. Add the stock, bring to the boil and allow to simmer for 5 minutes. Add the Chinese broccoli and bring to the boil for 2 minutes.

In the meantime, place the egg noodles in a bowl and pour over boiling water from the kettle. Drain the noodles after 2 minutes and add to the soup. Add the soy sauce and chilli, and spoon over the spiced beancurd and bean sprouts. Sprinkle with the spring onions and serve.

Vegetarian Pizza

This pizza is made with a home-made pizza base. As an alternative to making your own, you can either buy some bread dough from a baker or buy a ready-made pizza base from a supermarket or gourmet food shop.

MAKES 2 LARGE PIZZAS OR 8 SMALL PIZZAS

2 zucchinis, sliced lengthwise

1 small eggplant, cut into rounds

2 tablespoons olive oil

200 g (7 oz) mushrooms, sliced

100 g (3½ oz) baby spinach leaves, washed

1 quantity of plain pizza dough (p. 69)

2 cloves garlic, finely chopped

1 teaspoon finely chopped fresh thyme

freshly ground black pepper

a pinch of chilli pepper

8 tablespoons Italian-style tomato sauce, bottled or home-made (p. 210)

100 g (3½ oz) grated low-fat mozzarella

8–12 canned or bottled artichoke hearts, halved

8 Greek olives, pitted and halved

Brush the zucchini and eggplant with a little olive oil and cook on a hot grill or in a non-stick frying pan until soft. Transfer to a plate. Grill or pan-fry the mushrooms until soft. Transfer the mushrooms to a plate. Cook the spinach until soft.

Preheat the oven to 250°C (500°F).

Cut the pizza dough according to the number of pizzas you are preparing. Form the dough into balls and roll out into round pizza bases of about 1 cm (⅓ in) thickness or less. The dough can be stretched by pulling it gently. Place the pizza bases on greased oven trays.

In a small bowl mix the remaining olive oil with the garlic and thyme. Season with a little pepper and a pinch of chilli pepper. Brush the dough with this seasoned oil and spread a little tomato sauce on top. Sprinkle some of the cheese over the top and add the cooked spinach, mushrooms, zucchinis, eggplant and artichokes. Sprinkle with the remaining cheese and press in the olive halves.

Cook the pizzas in the preheated oven for about 15–20 minutes until the base is dry and lightly browned underneath.

Stir-fried spiced beancurd with young beans

You will find spiced beancurd in the refrigerated section at Asian foodstores. It usually comes in vacuum-packed sachets containing 4 or 6 squares of beancurd. Garlic chives are also readily available from Asian foodstores. The quantities of vegetables here can be easily varied according to your taste.

SERVES 2

1/2 tablespoon peanut oil

250 g (9 oz) fresh young beans, topped, tailed and cut diagonally into 3 cm (1 1/2 in) pieces

2 tablespoons water

2 squares spiced beancurd, cut into matchstick-size pieces

1/4 cup garlic chives, cut into 3 cm (1 1/2 in) pieces

1/3 of a small red hot chilli, finely sliced

1/2 teaspoon sugar

1/2 tablespoon light soy sauce

Heat a wok and add the oil. Add the beans and stir-fry for 10 seconds. Add the water, cover with a lid and steam-cook for about 2 minutes.

Stir in the spiced beancurd, garlic chives and chilli, and stir-fry for about 30 seconds. Add the sugar and soy sauce, stir-fry for about 1 minute and serve.

Polenta with olives & basil

Polenta, a finely ground cornmeal, is especially popular in Italy. Traditional polenta takes about 30 minutes to cook, but instant polenta, which is ready in minutes, is great for busy people. A popular way to serve polenta is to top it with fresh tomato sauce and a little grated cheese. Grill it until the cheese melts.

SERVES 4

600 ml (2 1/2 cups) water

1/4 teaspoon salt

150 g (5 oz) instant polenta

8 black olives, pitted and sliced

2 tablespoons finely sliced basil

1/2 tablespoon olive oil *or* butter

freshly ground black pepper

Preheat the oven to 220°C (450°F).

Line a small roasting tray with oven paper.

Bring the salted water to the boil. Slowly pour in the polenta, lower the heat and stir until the polenta is well mixed and has thickened. Stir in the olives, basil and half the oil. Season with pepper.

Pour the polenta into a roasting tray and spread it out to a thickness of about 2 cm (3/4 in). It does not matter if the base of the tray is not fully covered. Pour over the remaining oil and bake in a preheated oven for 5 minutes – longer if you like it dry. Serve immediately.

Couscous with vegetables

Couscous is a coarse wheat semolina that is a staple of North African cuisine. It is really like pasta, and usually comes in packets already partly cooked. The cooking instructions usually say to add the couscous to hot water for a few minutes, but I prefer to finish the cooking by steaming as it gives a lighter, fluffier grain. Harissa is a hot chilli paste available from good delis and food stores. This preparation is beautifully spicy.

SERVES 4

2 medium carrots, peeled and halved crosswise

2 turnips, peeled and halved

1 red capsicum, quartered and seeded

2 zucchinis, halved crosswise

3 tomatoes, quartered

1 tablespoon tomato paste

1 teaspoon harissa *or* chilli paste

1 teaspoon ground cummin

1 clove garlic, crushed

1 tablespoon olive oil

salt and freshly ground black pepper

400 g (14 oz) can chickpeas, drained

2–3 silverbeet leaves *or* a handful of spinach, shredded

300 g (11 oz) couscous

a few sprigs of coriander

In a large saucepan place the carrots, turnips, capsicum, zucchinis, tomatoes, tomato paste, harissa, cummin, garlic, and olive oil. Cover with water and season with salt and pepper. Bring to the boil and cook for 10 minutes.

Add the drained chickpeas and silverbeet, and cook for a further 10 minutes.

Place the couscous in a fine-mesh strainer and run cold water over it for a few minutes. Place a damp towel or muslin over the perforated compartment of your steamer and put the wet couscous over the cloth. Bring some water in the steamer base to the boil, and steam the couscous, uncovered, for 10–15 minutes or until the grains are soft. Stir with a fork to separate the grains.

Place the couscous on a dish and the vegetables and liquid separately in a serving bowl. Garnish with sprigs of coriander. Serve from the centre of the table for all to help themselves.

Tomato & spicy bean tartlets on filo

To save time, cook the base of these tartlets several hours before
your meal. Other vegetables such as mushrooms or capsicum can be
used in place of the tomato. Borlotti beans are ideal for this dish.

SERVES 6

4 sheets filo pastry

2 tablespoons olive oil

½ cup Italian-style tomato sauce,
bottled or home-made (p. 210)

3 black olives, pitted and chopped

salt and freshly ground black pepper

1 cup cooked beans, drained

¼ teaspoon ground cummin

¼ teaspoon chilli paste

1 tablespoon coriander leaves,
finely sliced

3 Roma tomatoes, finely sliced

2 small zucchinis, finely sliced

Preheat the oven to 180°C (350°F).

Line a greased baking sheet with one sheet of filo
pastry. Brush the pastry with a little oil and place a
second pastry sheet on top. Do likewise with the third
and fourth pastry sheets, brushing each layer with
oil. Cut the pastry into 6 equal rectangles.

In a small bowl, mix the tomato sauce with the olives
and a little pepper. Thinly spread a little of this
tomato preparation in the centre of each pastry
rectangle, leaving an edge of about 1 cm (⅓ in).
Bake the pastry in the preheated oven until the base
of the pastry is lightly browned. This takes about
10–15 minutes.

Blend the cooked beans to a purée with
1 tablespoon of the olive oil, the cummin and
chilli paste. Season to taste. Spread this bean
paste over the cooked pastry, sprinkle with coriander
and top with the tomato and zucchini slices in an
attractive overlapping pattern. Place the tartlets in
the preheated oven for about 10 minutes until the
tomato is hot and soft. Serve immediately.

pasta, noo

These foods are currently enjoying great popularity and it is a good thing for they provide us with long-lasting energy and are low in fat. Hence we often hear of sportspeople eating a dish of pasta before a performance. These foods are also among the easies and most popular for children to learn to cook. A bowl of plain pasta, noodle and rice, however, is not a meal in itself, and it is important to serve vegetables and a form of protein with it. Avoid eating pasta with sauces high in fat, such as those containing butter, cream, cheese or oil. And remember that pasta goes really well with fresh herbs, tomato sauce, garlic and vegetables.

dles & RICE

Always cook pasta in a large quantity of lightly salted boiling water. Read the cooking instructions on the pack or ask the people you buy fresh pasta from about cooking times.

Many varieties of noodles are available fresh or dried from Asian foodstores. Most dried noodles need only a few minutes' cooking in boiling water. Fresh noodles and some thinner dried noodles need only be reheated or soaked in hot water for 2 minutes. I have provided instructions on how to cook rice in this section, or you may follow the instructions on the pack.

Pasta.

This is the basic technique for cooking pasta. The cooking time for fresh or dry pasta varies from one brand to another so you need to read the packet instructions or ask the pasta seller for advice. If serving pasta as an accompaniment, season it with a little olive oil or butter and add grated parmesan.

SERVES 2 AS A MAIN COURSE

¼ teaspoon salt

3 litres water

1 teaspoon olive oil (optional)

200 g (7 oz) dry pasta *or* 250 g
   (9 oz) fresh pasta

In a large pot, bring the salted cold water to the boil. When boiling, add the oil and pasta, and return to the boil. Stir occasionally to prevent the pasta from sticking. Fresh pasta takes 2–5 minutes, while dry pasta takes 8–12 minutes.

Test the pasta by taking a piece with a pair of tongs. Cool briefly under the tap and bite into it. The pasta should be just a little firm in the centre – the Italians call this 'al dente'.

Once cooked, add about a cup of cold water to pasta and drain it in a colander, shaking out any excess water. Season with your favourite sauce or herb, and serve immediately.

Penne with mexican bean sauce

Penne is a cylindrical pasta that is very popular in Italy and all over the world. This dish is a main course and I like to serve it with a green salad.

SERVES 4

400 g (14 oz) penne

salt and freshly ground black pepper

1 tablespoon olive oil

½ brown onion, finely chopped

½ teaspoon cummin seeds

½ small chilli, finely sliced

1½ cups Italian-style tomato sauce,
   bottled *or* home-made (p. 210)

400 g (14 oz) can cannellini beans *or*
   other beans of your choice

a few sprigs of coriander *or* parsley,
   finely chopped (optional)

Cook the penne in a large pot of salted boiling water until al dente. This usually takes between 9–11 minutes. Drain.

Meanwhile, heat half of the oil in a non-stick pan. Add the onion and cook for 4 minutes over low heat. Add the cummin seeds and chilli, and stir-fry for 1 minute. Add the tomato sauce and drained beans and bring to a simmer.

Toss the drained penne with the bean sauce. Season with salt and pepper and stir in the remaining oil. Sprinkle with coriander or parsley before serving.

Macaroni with tuna & vegetables

This is one of those family dishes where you can use up any remaining vegetables you have in the fridge.

SERVES 2

about 200 g (7 oz) macaroni

1 cup broccoli, cut into small florets

½ teaspoon olive oil

6 mushrooms, sliced

2 tomatoes, diced

½ clove garlic, finely chopped

1 tablespoon finely sliced basil

200 g (7 oz) can of tuna in oil, drained and flaked

freshly ground black pepper

Bring a pot of lightly salted water to the boil and cook the macaroni in boiling water until al dente.

Place the broccoli in a bowl and cover with boiling water from the kettle. Drain after 2 minutes.

Heat the oil in a non-stick saucepan and cook the mushrooms for 2 minutes. Add the broccoli and stir gently. Add the tomatoes, cover and cook for about 3 minutes.

Mix the drained pasta with the vegetables, garlic, basil and tuna, and season with black pepper. Serve while hot.

Butterfly pasta with pumpkin & pinenuts

You can use another type of pasta in this dish if you wish. Try serving it with a green salad. Toast the pinenuts carefully under the grill until they just begin to brown.

SERVES 2

200 g (7 oz) pumpkin flesh, cut into small pieces

about 200 g (7 oz) butterfly pasta

salt and freshly ground black pepper

½ tablespoon olive oil

½ clove garlic, finely chopped

2 tablespoons chopped parsley

1 tablespoon pinenuts, toasted

1 tablespoon freshly grated parmesan

Place the pumpkin in a saucepan with a little water, cover and steam the pumpkin until soft. Alternatively, microwave until cooked.

Meanwhile, cook the pasta in a large volume of lightly salted boiling water.

Mash the cooked pumpkin and stir in the olive oil, garlic, parsley and a little salt and pepper to taste.

Gently toss the drained pasta with the pumpkin purée and serve sprinkled with pinenuts and grated parmesan.

Ravioli with spinach & olives

Many pasta shops make beautiful ravioli as well as other pasta parcels, like agnolotti. They are filled with meat, spinach and ricotta, mushrooms, pumpkin – the choice is wide. Read the packet instructions carefully for cooking times or ask your shopkeeper for advice.

SERVES 2

3 litres water

salt and freshly ground black pepper

350 g (12½ oz) fresh ravioli *or* 300 g (11 oz) dry ravioli

200 g (7 oz) young spinach leaves

1 tomato, diced

½ tablespoon olive oil

4 olives, pitted and finely sliced

1 tablespoon parmesan shavings or grated parmesan

If necessary, separate ravioli squares from one another. Bring the salted water to the boil. Add the pasta and stir gently. Cook the pasta until soft. Fresh ravioli takes 5–10 minutes, depending on the type used, while dry ravioli takes 10–18 minutes. Drain.

Cook the spinach in a covered saucepan until soft. (It cooks in its own steam.) Drain and season with a little salt and pepper.

Place the spinach on plates and divide the ravioli between them. Scatter over the diced tomato and drizzle the oil over the ravioli. Season with salt and pepper, top with olives and shavings of parmesan, and serve.

Spaghetti with chicken & eggplant

Be creative with this dish, and add vegetables and herbs of your choice. Make sure the chicken and vegetables are ready before the spaghetti.

SERVES 2

½ tablespoon olive oil

1 large chicken fillet, skinned and finely sliced

1 medium eggplant, diced

about 150 g (3½ oz) spaghetti

salt and freshly ground black pepper

about 100 g (3½ oz) baby spinach leaves

1 tomato, diced

1 clove garlic, finely chopped

1 tablespoon finely sliced basil or parsley

2 tablespoons grated parmesan

Heat half of the oil in a non-stick pan and brown the chicken pieces for 1 minute. Transfer to a plate.

Add the remaining oil to the pan and, on high heat, cook the eggplant until soft.

In the meantime, cook the spaghetti in a large quantity of salted boiling water.

When the eggplant is soft, add the spinach and cook until it has softened also. Stir in the tomato, garlic and basil or parsley, and season with salt and pepper.

Toss the drained spaghetti with the vegetables and serve sprinkled with a little grated parmesan.

Bolognese sauce

The vegetables in this sauce impart lots of flavour to the dish. Use very fresh mince.
The secret of a good bolognese is long slow cooking, and ideally it should cook for 2 hours.
Of course, you can reduce the cooking time if you're in a hurry but the sauce won't be as
flavoursome. The sauce will keep in the fridge for 2 to 3 days or frozen in a freezer
bag or air-tight container for up to 2 months.

SERVES 4

1 tablespoon olive oil

1 lean rasher bacon, diced

½ tablespoon chopped fresh thyme

1 small brown onion, peeled and finely
 diced

1 medium carrot, peeled and finely diced

2 sticks celery, peeled and finely diced

300 g (11 oz) lean ground beef

1 tablespoon plain flour

1 tablespoon plain tomato paste

½ cup red wine

2 cloves garlic, crushed

2 cups Italian-style tomato sauce, bottled
 or home-made (p. 210)

salt and freshly ground black pepper

Heat the oil in a saucepan and on medium heat fry
the bacon, thyme, onion, carrot and celery for about
5 minutes. Increase the heat and add the meat to pan.
Cook for a few minutes, stirring occasionally. Stir in the
flour and tomato paste. Stir in the wine and bring to the
boil. Add the garlic and tomato sauce. Season and stir
well. Lower the heat and bring to a simmer.

Cover and cook slowly for 1–2 hours. Stir occasionally
to prevent burning or sticking, and add a little boiling
water if you feel the sauce becoming too thick at any
stage. Alternatively, you can cook the sauce in a covered
casserole dish in the oven at 150°C (300°F) for about
1–2 hours.

Serve with your favourite pasta cooked al dente.

chef's note

This is a good
example of a dis
that takes little
time to cook.

Chinese egg noodles with vegetables

Prepare this dish using your favourite vegetables. Broccoli, cabbage and spinach work especially well. The Chinese egg noodles (chow-mein noodles) are readily available from Asian foodstores.

SERVES 2

3 sprigs of Chinese broccoli, cut diagonally into 4 cm (about 1¾ in) pieces

200 g (7 oz) Chinese egg noodles

½ tablespoon peanut *or* canola oil

1 slice ginger, left whole

½ clove garlic, crushed

1 rasher lean bacon, finely sliced (optional)

100 g (3½ oz) bean sprouts

½ tablespoon low-salt soy sauce

about 6 cherry tomatoes, quartered

½ small red chilli, finely sliced (optional)

2 spring onions, chopped

Place the Chinese broccoli in a bowl and cover with boiling water. Drain after 4 minutes.

Place the noodles in a bowl and cover with boiling water. Drain after 3 minutes.

Heat a wok and, when hot, add the oil. Stir in the ginger, garlic and bacon, and fry for 10 seconds. Add the Chinese broccoli and stir-fry for about 2 minutes. Add the bean sprouts and stir-fry for 1 minute. Add the drained noodles, soy sauce, cherry tomatoes and chilli. Stir gently to mix well. When heated through, serve sprinkled with spring onions.

Indonesian stir-fry vegetables with mince & noodles

This is one of the first dishes my wife, Angie, cooked for
me almost twenty years ago. It is now a family favourite.

SERVES 4

150 g (5 oz) dry Asian
noodles *or* spaghetti

1 egg

2 tablespoons water

1 tablespoon peanut oil

½ onion, diced

1 rasher lean bacon, trimmed
and diced

1 clove garlic, chopped

150 g (5 oz) lean minced meat

3 sticks celery, diced

½ capsicum, seeded and diced

4 small carrots, diced

⅛ cabbage, shredded

½ teaspoon chilli sauce or to taste

½ tablespoon soy sauce

freshly ground black pepper

Cook the noodles for 3 minutes in boiling water. Strain
and refresh under cold running water. Drain. If using
spaghetti, cook according to the intructions on the
packet.

Beat the egg with the water. Brush a small non-stick
frying pan with oil and quickly scramble the egg.
Transfer to a plate.

Pour half of the remaining oil in a hot wok and, when
the oil is hot, fry the onion on high heat until just brow
around the edges. Transfer to a bowl, and fry the bac
until crisp. Place with the onion.

Add the garlic to the wok and stir in the mince. Fry un
the meat is browned, stirring to remove any lumps, the
transfer to a bowl.

Heat the remaining oil in a wok and add the celery,
capsicum, carrots and cabbage. Stir-fry until the
vegetables soften. If the mixture starts to burn, pour
a few tablespoons of water down the side of the wok.

Return the onion, bacon, egg, meat, and noodles to t
wok. Season with chilli, soy sauce and pepper. Toss we
to heat through and distribute the flavours. Serve.

Singapore-style noodles

Young men seem to love this dish. You will need to buy some Chinese roast pork (*char siew*), which is sold in strips by weight in some Chinese take-away shops.

SERVES 2

100 g (3½ oz) fresh Chinese egg noodles

1 tablespoon oil

1 teaspoon grated ginger

1 clove garlic, chopped

1 teaspoon curry powder

1 stick celery, finely sliced

1 baby carrot, finely sliced

2 tablespoons water

½ cup cooked shrimps

100 g (3½ oz) Chinese roast pork, finely sliced

1 cup bean sprouts

1 hard-boiled egg, sliced

2 spring onions, finely sliced

1 tablespoon soy sauce

a few sprigs of coriander

Place the noodles in a bowl and cover with boiling water from the kettle. Drain after 2 minutes.

Heat the oil in a wok and stir-fry the ginger, garlic, curry powder, celery and carrot for about 1 minute. Add the water down the side of the wok to stop any scorching and stir-fry for a further minute. Add the shrimps and pork and stir-fry for about 30 seconds. Add the bean sprouts and stir-fry for 30 seconds. Gently toss in the noodles, egg and spring onions. Season with soy sauce and serve sprinkled with sprigs of coriander.

Stir-fried beef & broccoli with thin noodles

Here is a simple stir-fry dish for those who love Chinese food. Once you have mastered the technique of stir-frying, try adding other vegetables to vary the dish.

SERVES 2

½ tablespoon shaoshing (Chinese rice wine) *or* dry sherry

1 teaspoon cornflour

freshly ground black pepper

½ tablespoon cold water

200 g (7 oz) lean rump steak, cut across the grain into ½ cm (¼ in) slices

200 g (7 oz) broccoli, cut into florets

200 g (7 oz) thin, fresh egg noodles

1 tablespoon peanut oil

1 clove garlic, finely sliced

1 teaspoon grated ginger

½ tablespoon low-salt soy sauce

½ teaspoon sesame oil

In a medium bowl combine the wine, cornflour, pepper and water. Stir in the beef.

Place the broccoli in a bowl and pour over boiling water from the kettle. Drain after 2 minutes.

Place the egg noodles in a bowl and pour over boiling water from the kettle. Drain after 2 minutes.

Pour half of the peanut oil into a hot wok and when the oil is hot, stir-fry the broccoli for about 2 minutes until tender. Transfer the broccoli to a bowl.

Heat the remaining oil and stir in the garlic and ginger. Add the beef and stir-fry on high heat for about 20–30 seconds until it changes colour. Stir in the soy sauce, sesame oil, broccoli and noodles and heat through before serving.

Steamed Rice

Rice is popular with most people and is an excellent food for
people with wheat allergies. I use a long-grain rice such as basmati or jasmine.
It's essential to cook the rice in a saucepan with a tight-fitting lid.

SERVES 3

1 cup long-grain rice

1 ½ cups cold water

a pinch of salt

1 teaspoon peanut, canola *or* olive oil

Rinse the rice under running water and drain.

Place the water, salt and oil in a saucepan. Add the rice, bring to a simmer and cover the pan immediately with a tight-fitting lid. Cook on low heat for 17 minutes. The rice is now ready.

For brown rice, use 1 cup brown rice to 2 cups water and cook for about 40 minutes following the above method.

Risotto with chicken & vegetables

Cooked chicken meat from a leftover roast or boiled chicken is ideal for this dish.

SERVES 3

1 tablespoon olive oil

½ onion, finely chopped

½ carrot, finely chopped

10 cm (4 in) stick celery,
   finely chopped

3 cups chicken stock (p. 204)

1 cup risotto rice (short, round grain)

8 mushrooms, finely chopped

¼ cup dry white wine

1½ cups diced, cooked chicken meat

2 tablespoons freshly grated parmesan

salt and freshly ground black pepper

1 tablespoon chopped parsley

Heat the oil in a medium saucepan and gently fry the onion, carrot and celery for about 3 minutes.

Bring the chicken stock to the boil, then reduce the heat to keep it simmering while making the risotto.

Add the rice to the vegetables and mix well for about 1 minute. Stir in the mushrooms. Add the wine and about 1 cup of stock to the pan and bring to a gentle simmer, stirring all the time. Simmer until almost all the stock has been absorbed, then add another half a cup of stock. Keep adding the stock, a quarter of a cup at a time, stirring all the time, until the rice is cooked but still a little firm in the centre. You may either have a little stock left over or you may have run out, in which case add some boiling water.

Add the diced chicken to the pan 2 minutes before the rice is ready. While stirring, add the parmesan and season with a little salt and pepper. Taste a few grains of rice to check if it is cooked. At this point, the preparation will be creamy but not runny. Cover the risotto with a lid and rest it for about 3 minutes before serving. In all, the cooking takes about 18–20 minutes.

Sprinkle with parsley just before serving.

Paella

This Spanish dish is popular with people from the Mediterranean region who see it as a complete family meal, served with plenty of rice and vegetables and just a little meat or seafood to flavour the dish. It is a treat and a great party dish to serve from the centre of the table.

SERVES 6–8

1 tablespoon olive oil

8 small drumsticks *or* other chicken pieces, fat and skin removed

1 small brown onion, diced

1 red capsicum, sliced

2 tomatoes, chopped

1 cup shelled peas

1¼ cups short-grain rice

3 cups cold water *or* chicken stock (p. 204)

salt and freshly ground black pepper

2 pinches of saffron

½ hot chilli

12 mussels, washed and de-bearded

½ cup dry white wine

about 8 (or more) green prawns

2 tablespoons chopped parsley

Heat the oil in a wide pan or casserole dish, and brown the chicken pieces. Add the onion and stir for 2 minutes. Then add the capsicum, tomatoes, peas, rice and water or stock. Bring to a simmer, season with salt, pepper, saffron and chilli. Stir gently to combine the spices. Cover and simmer for about 20 minutes.

Place the washed mussels and white wine in a pan and bring to the boil. Cover and cook for a few minutes until the mussel shells have opened.

Add the prawns to the rice and chicken mixture and cook for a further 5 minutes. Add a little extra water or strained mussel juice to the rice towards the end of the cooking if it becomes too dry.

Serve the paella in the pan or dish it was cooked in, with the opened mussels on top. Sprinkle with the parsley and serve.

Chinese broccoli with oyster sauce

I really love Chinese broccoli, and this simple dish is wonderful either with grilled or pan-fried fish or chicken, or even with noodles.

SERVES 3

about 400 g (14 oz) Chinese broccoli

1 tablespoon peanut oil

1 tablespoon oyster sauce

1/2 teaspoon sugar

Wash the Chinese broccoli and cut the long stalks in half.

Bring a medium saucepan of water to the boil. Add the oil and broccoli, and after the water has returned to the boil, cook broccoli for 1 minute. Drain, reserving a little of the cooking liquid, and transfer the broccoli to a serving dish.

In a small bowl mix together the oyster sauce, sugar and 1 tablespoon of the cooking liquid from the broccoli. Pour this over the Chinese broccoli and serve immediately.

Ratatouille

This flavoursome vegetable dish can be served with fish, meat, pasta and eggs, and is even delicious cold.

SERVES 3

1 tablespoon olive oil

1/2 brown onion, diced

2 sprigs of thyme *or* parsley *or* 4 basil leaves

2 cloves garlic, chopped

1/2 red capsicum, cut into 2 cm (3/4 in) pieces

2 medium zucchinis, cut into 2 cm (3/4 in) pieces

1 small eggplant, cut into 2 cm (3/4 in) pieces

3 tomatoes, diced

salt and freshly ground black pepper

Heat the oil in a non-stick saucepan and stir-fry the onion and thyme for about 2 minutes on medium heat.

Add the garlic and capsicum and stir-fry for another 2 minutes. Add the zucchini and eggplant and stir well for 1 minute before adding the tomatoes. Season with a little salt and pepper, cover, and cook for 10–20 minutes, depending on how well done you like the vegetables.

Artichokes Provençale

I particularly love this dish. Artichokes are a superb vegetable and the
result here is quite exotic. The most demanding part of the dish is in the preparation:
you have to trim away the leaves of the artichoke until you reach the heart.

SERVES 3–4

1 litre cold water

½ lemon

6 large artichokes

1 tablespoon olive oil

1 small onion, finely chopped

1 teaspoon coriander seeds

12 fennel seeds

1 teaspoon tomato paste

½ glass dry white wine

4 medium tomatoes, chopped

3–4 sprigs of parsley, chopped

an extra 2 slices of lemon, quartered

salt and freshly ground black pepper

Pour about 1 litre cold water into a bowl and place the half lemon into it.

Using a very sharp knife, cut off the artichoke stalks. Cut through the top part of the artichokes, leaving about 3½ cm (about 1⅓ in) of the base. Trim away the remaining leaves, leaving only the heart. Using a spoon, scoop out the choke (the hairy part) from the centre of the heart. When all the hearts are trimmed and clean, place them in the water and rub them with the lemon to prevent discolouring.

Heat the oil in a pan and gently fry the onion for 3–4 minutes. Cut each artichoke heart into 6 pieces. Add to the pan and stir for 1 minute. Add the coriander and fennel seeds, stir in the tomato paste, wine, and the chopped tomatoes, parsley sprigs and pieces of lemon. Season, cover the pan and cook, stirring occasionally, for about 15 minutes or until the artichokes are soft.

Serve hot or cold. I enjoy it best cold myself.

Grilled vegetables

Grilled vegetables can be cooked on a cast-iron grill or on the barbecue. They are delicious as part of an antipasto selection, as a garnish for fish or meat or as a sandwich filling.

SERVES ABOUT 4

2 tablespoons olive oil

1 teaspoon freshly chopped thyme

1 clove garlic, finely chopped (optional)

1 eggplant, cut into 1 cm (1/3 in) slices lengthwise

2 zucchinis, cut into 1 cm (1/3 in) slices lengthwise

2 large mushrooms, cut into 1 cm (1/3 in) slices

1 red capsicum, cut into about 8 long strips

salt and freshly ground black pepper

Mix two-thirds of the oil with the thyme and brush the vegetables on both sides. This can be done several hours in advance. Mix the remaining oil with the garlic.

Heat the grill or barbecue. Place the vegetables on the grill and cook for 1 minute. Move the vegetables a quarter of a turn to form a criss-cross pattern and cook for a further minute. Turn over and cook the second side, taking care not to burn the vegetables. Brush lightly with the garlic oil and season with a little salt and pepper before serving.

chef's note

t is important before starting to ensure hat the grill or barbecue is very clean.

FISH &

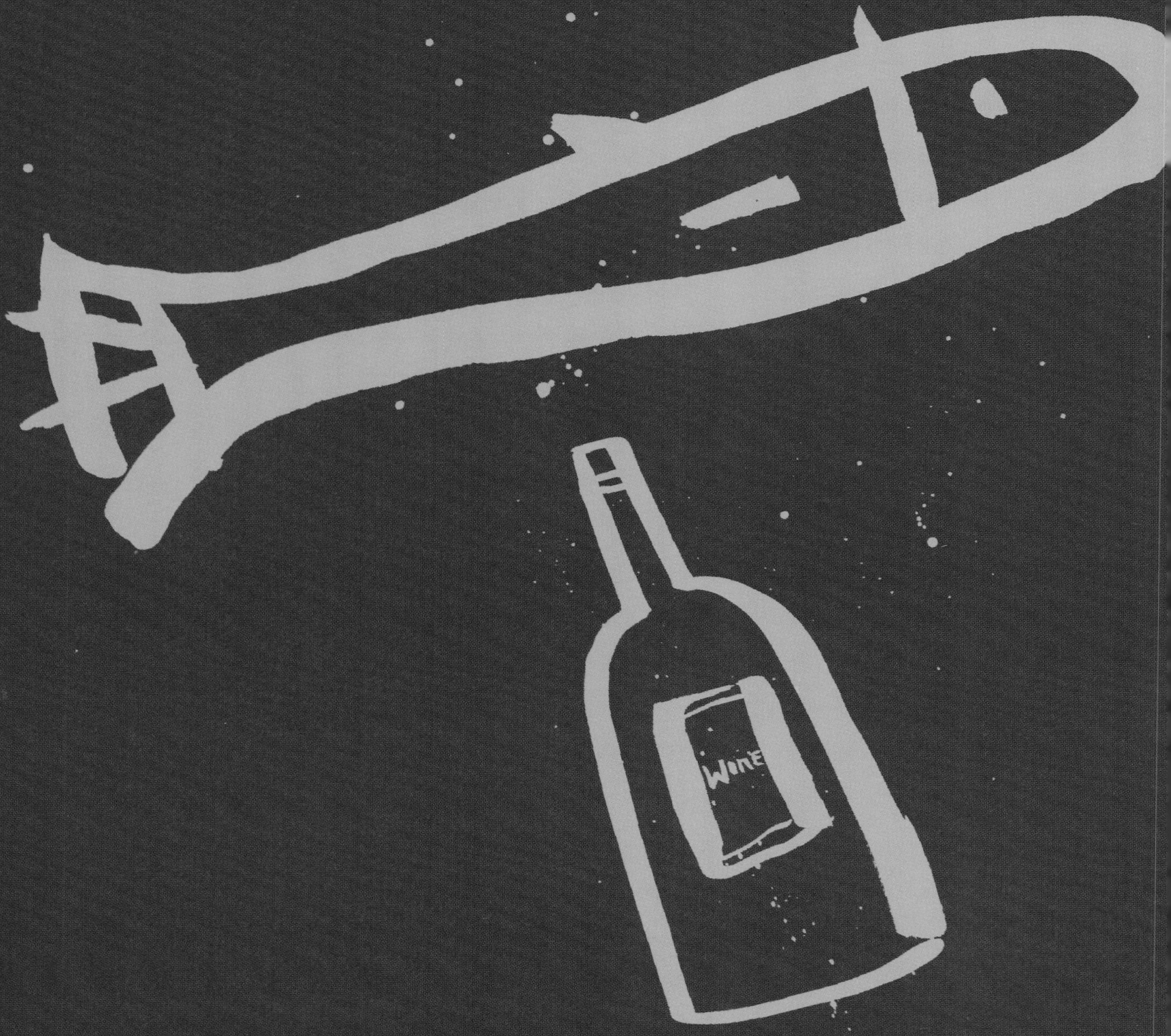

SEAFOOD

Much research has been done on the nutritional value of fish, and the results are always positive, especially when the fish has been cooked in little or no oil at all. While most varieties of fish are naturally low in fat, they do contain a fatty acid known as omega-3, which has been associated with helping lower blood fat, reduce blood pressure and prevent the blood from clotting too readily. My experience has taught me that men, especially those who love to go fishing, generally feel more comfortable handling fish than women do. So maybe the men could become the family fish cooks!

Fish takes little time to cook. A 3 cm (1½ in) thick fish fillet takes 5 to 6 minutes (2½ to 3 minutes per side) in a non-stick pan over medium heat. A fish cutlet takes about the same length of time. Fish fillets and cutlets can be easily cooked under the grill for about 2½ to 3 minutes on each side. Whole fish will take a little longer. Whole fish, fish fillets and cutlets can also be cooked in the oven in a baking tray. Fish retains its lovely flavour when simply steamed in a little liquid (water, stock or wine) or cooked with vegetables (tomato, mushrooms or celery). Whole fish are lovely pan-fried or baked; their cooking times depend on their shape and weight. Enjoy fish two or three times a week.

Pan-fried fish fillets with asparagus & mushrooms

Fish, mushrooms and asparagus go well together. Ask your fishmonger for the freshest fish available. This dish works well with blue eye, blue grenadier or perch.

SERVES 2

about 6–8 asparagus spears, cut diagonally into 4 cm (1 1/2 in) pieces

1/2 tablespoon olive oil

2 x 150 g (5 oz) fresh fish fillets

salt and freshly ground black pepper

200 g (7 oz) mushrooms, sliced

2 slices of lemon (garnish)

2 spring onions, finely sliced (garnish)

Bring cold water to the boil in a medium saucepan and boil or steam the asparagus until cooked. Drain.

Heat the olive oil in a non-stick frying pan and cook the fish, skinned side first, for 2 1/2 minutes. Turn the fish over and cook for about 2 1/2 minutes on the other side. Season with a little salt and pepper, transfer to a plate and cover with foil to keep warm.

Add mushrooms to the pan and stir-fry until soft. Stir in the asparagus and season to taste. Place the vegetables around the fish. Garnish with the lemon slices and spring onions, and serve.

chef's note

Dill is a classic w
salmon, but you
can also try cher
tarragon or basi

Panfried Salmon with dill & vegetables .

The vegetables in this dish can be steamed or microwaved, and if you wish, serve the dish with steamed or baked potatoes. The salmon can be replaced by another fish of your choice.

SERVES 2

4 baby carrots, peeled

1 small swede *or* turnip, peeled and quartered

100 g (3½ oz) beans, topped and tailed

1 tablespoon olive oil

2 x 120 g (4 oz) salmon fillets, skin on or off

1 tomato, halved

salt and freshly ground black pepper

3 sprigs of dill, 1 sprig chopped and the others left whole

2 lemon wedges

Bring water to the boil in a steamer. Add the carrots and swede, cover and cook for 4 minutes. Add the beans and steam until just cooked.

Heat half the oil in a non-stick pan and pan-fry the salmon and tomato halves for about 2½–3 minutes on each side. Season with a little salt and pepper.

Toss the steamed vegetables with the remaining olive oil and chopped dill, and season with pepper.

Sprinkle the lemon juice over the fish and serve with the vegetables and the sprig of dill.

Fish fillet with tomato & olives in foil

Serve this easy dish with steamed or microwaved broccoli or French beans, or with a green salad. Ask your fishmonger for the freshest fish fillets available. You will need a 30 cm (12 in) square of foil.

SERVES 1

a little olive oil

1 small tomato, cut into 1 cm (1/3 in) slices

a sprig of parsley or about 4 basil leaves

150 g (5 oz) fish fillet

freshly ground black pepper

2 black olives, pitted and finely sliced

1 lemon wedge

Preheat the oven to 200°C (400°F).

Brush the centre of the foil with a little olive oil.

Place half the tomato slices in the centre of the foil and place the parsley and fish fillet on top. Season with a little pepper and top with olives and the remaining tomato slices. Squeeze a few drops of lemon juice over the fish and close the foil to seal the contents. Place on a tray in the preheated oven and cook for about 10 minutes.

To serve, carefully open the fish parcel (the steam escaping from the foil can burn) and transfer the contents to a plate. Spoon over the cooking juices and accompany with vegetables of your choice.

John dory with chinese broccoli

John Dory is a superb firm fish, easy to handle and cook. You may need to order it from a reliable fishmonger. As an alternative, use barramundi or blue eye.

SERVES 2

about 400 g (14 oz) Chinese broccoli

1 teaspoon peanut oil

2 x 150 g (5 oz) John Dory fillets, skinned

1/2 tablespoon low-salt soy sauce

juice of 1/4 lemon

2 spring onions, cut into 1 cm (1/3 in) pieces

freshly ground black pepper (optional)

Trim away the hard broccoli stalks and wash well. Bring a saucepan of cold water to the boil and cook the broccoli for 3 minutes. Drain.

Heat the oil in a non-stick frying pan. Cook the fish for 2½ minutes, turn, and cook the other side for 2½ minutes. Transfer the fillets to a serving plate.

Add soy sauce and lemon juice to the pan. Toss in the spring onions and broccoli, and stir to distribute the flavours.

Place the broccoli around the fish and spoon over the sauce. Season with black pepper and serve.

Trout with Almonds

To prepare this delicate dish use a large, preferably non-stick, frying pan that will hold the trout comfortably. Otherwise, cook the fish on the barbecue or under the grill. I like to eat the fish first on its own followed by a separate salad or vegetable. It makes an ideal Sunday lunch.

SERVES 2

1 tablespoon flaked almonds

2 small trout, scaled

a little plain flour

salt and freshly ground black pepper

2 tablespoons olive oil

2 tablespoons chopped parsley

juice of ½ lemon

Lightly brown the almonds under the grill or in a hot oven. Watch them carefully – they burn very quickly.

Briefly rinse the scaled trout under cold running water and pat dry with kitchen paper. Place the flour on a plate and season with salt and pepper. Coat the fish lightly with flour.

Heat about two-thirds of the oil in a pan. Place the trout carefully in the pan and cook for about 4 minutes on each side.

Carefully transfer the trout to serving plates and sprinkle with toasted almonds and chopped parsley. Sprinkle the fish with the remaining oil and lemon juice and serve immediately.

Marinated Sardine fillets with tomato sauce

Many fishmongers now sell sardines that have already been filleted. For this dish, buy sardines on the day you eat them as they need to be very fresh. The tomato sauce may be prepared the day before and it is best to marinate the sardines for between 2 and 6 hours.

SERVES 4

⅓ cup freshly squeezed lemon juice (about 3 lemons)

about 12 fennel seeds or a pinch of aniseed

8–12 sardines, filleted

a handful of greens, such as rocket

1 cup Italian-style tomato sauce, bottled or home-made (p. 210)

1 tablespoon extra-virgin olive oil

8 coriander seeds, crushed

about 4 peppercorns, crushed

a few sprigs of fresh herbs, such as dill, parsley or chervil

Place the lemon juice and fennel seeds in a deep dish. Line the dish with sardines and shake to allow the juice to cover the fish. Refrigerate for at least 2 hours.

Drain the sardines and place on top of the greens in the centre of four large plates. Spoon the tomato sauce around the fish and drizzle over a little olive oil. Sprinkle with crushed coriander and peppercorns, and top with fresh herbs. Enjoy the dish with fresh bread.

Sardines with pumpkin & brussels sprout purée

I consider sardines a real treat and yet they are one of the least expensive fish available. It is best to buy them very fresh and eat them on the same day. Use a non-stick pan to cook the sardines.

SERVES 2

about 150 g (5 oz) brussels sprouts, trimmed and halved

about 150 g (5 oz) pumpkin, peeled and cut into 1 cm (1/3 in) thick pieces

salt and freshly ground black pepper

a pinch of cayenne pepper

2 teaspoons butter

1 tablespoon olive oil

12–14 sardines, gutted and cleaned

2 lemon wedges

Bring water to the boil in a steamer. Add the sprouts and pumpkin to the steamer and cook until soft. In either a blender or food mill, separately blend the sprouts and pumpkin to a purée and season each with a little salt, pepper, cayenne and 1 teaspoon each of butter.

Heat the oil in a non-stick frying pan and cook the sardines for 2 minutes on each side. Season with salt and pepper and serve sprinkled with lemon juice and accompanied by the puréed vegetables.

Tagliatelle marinara with vegetables

Adapt this dish to your taste by choosing your favourite seafood and pasta shape.

SERVES 2

200 g (7 oz) tagliatelle

200 g (7 oz) snowpeas, topped
   and tailed

1 tablespoon olive oil

4 green prawns, shelled and deveined

8 scallops, washed

100 g (3½ oz) firm fish fillets, cut into
bite-sized pieces

½ red capsicum, diced

1 tablespoon brandy (optional)

1 cup Italian-style tomato sauce,
   bottled or home-made (p. 210)

salt and freshly ground black pepper

a pinch of cayenne pepper

1 clove garlic, finely chopped

1 tablespoon finely shredded basil
   or parsley

Bring a large pot of lightly salted water to the boil and cook the pasta in boiling water until al dente.

Place the snowpeas in a bowl and pour over some boiling water from the kettle. After 2 minutes, drain.

Heat the olive oil in a non-stick pan and cook the prawns, scallops and fish for about 2 minutes. Transfer to a plate. Add the capsicum to the pan and stir-fry on medium heat for 2 minutes. Add the brandy and tomato sauce, and bring to the boil. Season with salt, pepper and cayenne. Mix the seafood, garlic and basil with the sauce and toss gently with the drained spaghetti and snowpeas. Serve immediately.

Stir-fried fish with bean sprouts & silverbeet

For this easy-to-prepare dish choose the freshest firm fish you can get your hands on and, if unsure as to freshness, ask your fishmonger for help. Barramundi, blue eye or gurnard work beautifully.

SERVES 2

300 g (11 oz) firm fresh fish fillets, cut into 1 cm (1/3 in) strips

1/2 tablespoon shaoshing wine (Chinese rice wine) *or* dry sherry

2 teaspoons cornflour

1/2 small egg white

4 cups cold water

1/2 tablespoon peanut oil

1 slice fresh ginger

1/2 clove garlic, finely sliced

about 100 g (3 1/2 oz) bean sprouts, washed and picked through

about 5 silverbeet leaves, stalks removed and shredded

1/2 teaspoon sesame oil

juice of 1/2 lemon

1/4 teaspoon chilli paste

1/2 tablespoon soy sauce

Mix the fish in a bowl with the wine, cornflour and egg white. Marinate for 20 minutes in the refrigerator.

Bring the water to the boil in a wok. Drop the fish strips into the boiling water and after 30 seconds tip the fish into a colander to drain.

Reheat the wok and add the oil. When the oil is hot, stir in the ginger and garlic, then immediately (otherwise the garlic will burn) add the bean sprouts and silverbeet. Stir-fry until soft. Stir in the sesame oil, lemon juice, chilli paste and soy sauce. Return the fish to the wok and gently mix with the vegetables. Heat through and serve immediately.

Chinese-style fish cutlets with spinach

Tell your fishmonger how you intend to cook the fish and allow him or her to help you choose the best and freshest fish for the task. If you wish, use a whole fish instead of cutlets.

SERVES 2

1 teaspoon peanut oil

1/2 teaspoon sesame oil

1 teaspoon honey

1/4 teaspoon chilli paste

1/2 clove garlic, finely chopped

1 teaspoon grated ginger

juice of 1/2 lemon

2 teaspoons low-salt soy sauce

2 x 120 g (4 oz) fish cutlets

about 300 g (11 oz) young spinach leaves

salt and freshly ground black pepper

1 teaspoon sesame seeds

2 spring onions, finely sliced

Preheat the oven to 200°C (400°F).

In a bowl, mix the peanut oil, half the sesame oil, honey, chilli paste, garlic, ginger, lemon juice and soy sauce.

Place the fish cutlets in a small oven dish and pour over the marinade. Turn the fish over to coat the other side. Place the dish in the preheated oven. After 5 minutes turn the fish over, cover with foil and cook for a further 5–10 minutes.

Wash the spinach and drain well. Heat the remaining sesame oil in a non-stick pan. Add the spinach, cover with a lid and cook for 3–4 minutes until the leaves have wilted. Season.

Place the spinach on a plate and sprinkle with sesame seeds. Put the fish on top, spoon over the sauce, sprinkle with spring onions and serve.

Curried flathead with coriander & celery

Use gurnard, mackerel or snapper if flathead is unavailable, but whether using whole fish or cutlets, a firm fish is preferable. If using fillets, reduce the cooking time. Bottled tamarind concentrate is available from Asian foodstores.

SERVES 2

600 g (1 ¼ lb) flathead

juice of ½ lemon

1 teaspoon tamarind concentrate

½ cup hot water

2 cm (¾ in) piece ginger, peeled

2 cloves garlic

½ cup fresh coriander leaves

½ small red chilli, or to taste

2 tablespoons peanut oil

½ small brown onion, chopped

¼ teaspoon cummin seeds

½ teaspoon ground cummin

1 teaspoon ground coriander

1 teaspoon turmeric

a pinch of chilli powder

freshly ground black pepper

4–5 sticks celery, peeled and cut into bite-sized pieces

Cut the fish into pieces, if you wish, and pour the lemon juice over the fish.

Dilute the tamarind in the hot water.

Blend the ginger, garlic, coriander leaves and red chilli to a purée.

Heat the oil in a large frying pan or wok. Add the onion and cook for about 4 minutes on low heat. Stir in the cummin seeds and cook for 1 minute before stirring in the ground cummin, coriander, turmeric, chilli powder and a little pepper. Cook for about 2 minutes. Add the ginger and coriander purée and cook for 1 minute. Add the diluted tamarind, bring to a simmer and cook for about 10 minutes.

Steam or microwave the celery until cooked.

Place the fish in the spicy sauce and shake the pan to allow the sauce to thoroughly coat the fish. Simmer for 3 minutes, turn the fish over and cook for another 3–5 minutes, depending on the thickness of the fish.

To serve, place the fish over the celery and spoon over the sauce. Serve immediately with steamed rice.

Salmon Tartlets on filo

This dish can be prepared with a fish other than salmon. Try fillets of red mullet or tuna and, if you wish, alter the seasoning to suit your taste or the occasion. Serve with a mixed green salad.

SERVES 6

4 sheets filo pastry

2 tablespoons olive oil

about ½ cup Italian-style tomato sauce, bottled or home-made (p. 210)

1 anchovy fillet, finely chopped

3 black olives, pitted and chopped

freshly ground black pepper

200 g (7 oz) salmon fillet, cut into 6 thin slices

a small sprig of lemon thyme, finely chopped

salt

about 6 green olives, finely chopped

a few sprigs of chervil

Preheat the oven to 180°C (350°F).

Line a baking sheet with one sheet of filo pastry. Brush the pastry with a little oil and place a second sheet of pastry on top. Do likewise with the third and fourth pastry sheets, brushing each sheet with a little oil.

Cut out 6 rounds of pastry by placing a saucer on top of the pastry and going round the edges of the saucer with the blade of a knife. Discard pastry around circles.

In a small bowl mix the tomato sauce with 1 teaspoon of the olive oil, the anchovy and olives, and season with black pepper. Thinly spread a little of this tomato preparation in the centre of each pastry round, leaving a 1 cm (⅓ in) edge. Bake the pastry rounds in the preheated oven until done. This takes about 10–15 minutes.

Coat the salmon with the remaining olive oil and lemon thyme and season with salt and pepper. Place the salmon slices on the cooked pastry rounds. Place the tartlets in the oven for a few minutes until the salmon just starts to change colour. Serve sprinkled with chopped green olives and a few sprigs of chervil.

Spicy stir-fried prawns on bok choy

Enjoy this dish either on its own or serve it as part of a Chinese meal. Most prawns available now have been frozen, so if you can't obtain fresh prawns choose prawns that are still frozen or just beginning to thaw at the time of purchase. Avoid soft-looking prawns with dark spots.

SERVES 2

12–18 green prawns, shelled and deveined

1 tablespoon shaoshing wine (Chinese rice wine) *or* dry sherry

1 tablespoon cornflour

½ small egg white

1½ tablespoons tomato sauce *or* ketchup

3 heads bok choy, halved

4 baby carrots, cut into small pieces

4 cups water

1 tablespoon peanut oil

1 clove garlic, finely chopped

½ tablespoon grated ginger

1 spring onion, very finely sliced

½ small red chilli, finely sliced

In a bowl, mix the prawns with half the rice wine, cornflour and egg white. Refrigerate for 30 minutes.

In another bowl mix the remaining wine and tomato sauce.

Wash the bok choy well. Bring a large saucepan of water to the boil and cook the bok choy and carrot pieces for 2 minutes. Drain.

In a wok bring the 4 cups of water to the boil. Drop in the marinated prawns and cook for 30 seconds until they change colour. Tip immediately into a colander and drain.

Reheat the wok and add half the oil to the wok. When the oil is hot, stir-fry the bok choy and carrots for 2 minutes. Transfer the vegetables to serving plates and keep warm. Heat the remaining oil and stir in the garlic, ginger and spring onion, and cook gently for 2 minutes. Stir in the wine and tomato mixture and the chilli. Return the prawns to the wok to reheat and coat with the sauce. Spoon the prawns and sauce over the bed of vegetables and serve immediately.

Tuna & Fennel casserole

Fennel, a vegetable which is usually available in autumn and winter, is very popular in Mediterranean countries for its aniseed flavour. This casserole is lovely served with steamed potatoes.

SERVES 2

1 medium globe fennel

1 tablespoon olive oil

2 tomatoes, sliced

1 clove garlic, crushed

4 sprigs of parsley, chopped

300 g (11 oz) tuna cutlet

salt and freshly ground black pepper

a sprig of thyme, finely chopped

1/2 glass dry white wine

Preheat the oven to 200°C (400°F).

Trim the fennel of any damaged leaves and trim the top. Cut the fennel into 1 cm (1/3 in) slices.

Place half the olive oil in an ovenproof pan. Top with half of the tomato slices, the garlic, half the parsley and the fennel. Place the fish on top and season with a little salt, pepper and thyme. Top with the remaining parsley, oil and tomato. Pour over the wine, cover with foil and a lid and bake in the preheated oven for about 30 minutes or until the fish and vegetables are soft and cooked through.

Scampi & leeks with a chive dressing

This is an entrée or light meal that those who love typically French flavours will enjoy. Leeks are a very popular vegetable in France – try to get the smallest leeks you can. If scampi are unavailable, use prawns.

SERVES 6

6 very small leeks

18 green scampi

a little plain flour

salt and freshly ground black pepper

2 tablespoons olive oil

1/2 tablespoon raspberry vinegar

2 tablespoons snipped chives

Wash the leeks and remove any damaged leaves. Steam, microwave or boil the leeks until just cooked, then cut into about 5 cm (2 in) lengths. Place on a serving platter.

Shell and devein the scampi (you may have to use a pair of scissors for this). Coat the scampi with a little flour and season with salt and pepper.

Heat half a tablespoon of oil in a non-stick frying pan and cook the scampi for 1 minute on both sides.

To make the dressing, mix the raspberry vinegar with the remaining olive oil, season with salt and pepper, and mix in the chives.

Serve the scampi and leeks immediately with the dressing spooned over.

Scallops, asparagus & Mesclun salad

Fresh scallops are a must for this special dish. Replace the scallops with prawns if you wish. Mesclun salad is a mix of leafy greens available from many greengrocers. If unavailable, substitute with baby spinach or other green leaves of your choice.

SERVES 6

about 18 asparagus spears

200 g (7 oz) Mesclun salad

2 shallots, finely chopped

½ tablespoon raspberry vinegar

about 2 tablespoons olive oil

salt and freshly ground black pepper

about 30 firm scallops

12 sprigs of chervil

2 tablespoons walnut flesh, cut into small pieces

Peel the asparagus spears and snap off the hard part at the base. Wash, then steam or microwave the asparagus until cooked.

Wash and dry the salad leaves.

In a salad bowl thoroughly combine the shallots, vinegar and 1 ½ tablespoons olive oil, and season with salt and pepper. Toss the asparagus and Mesclun in half the dressing.

Heat the remaining oil in a non-stick pan and pan-fry the scallops on either side for about 30 seconds.

Place the Mesclun and asparagus in the centre of a serving dish. Distribute the scallops around the salad and spoon over the remaining dressing. Dot with sprigs of chervil and walnuts, and serve.

The flavour of chicken is very popular and this tender meat can be prepared in hundreds of ways, as most herbs and spices seem to go well with it. Over the last ten years, poulterers have become quite creative in the variety of cuts they produce from a chicken. Many cuts are now available with or without the skin, on the bone or deboned, whole or diced, sliced or minced. It is preferable to trim all visible fat from the chicken or chicken pieces and to cook it without the skin. Chicken pieces must be used within two days of purchase, and if unsure about freshness, smell it. Your nose will let you know. Chicken casseroles with vegetables are popular and simple to prepare, and novice cooks will be thrilled with the results. Use a minimum of fat when cooking chicken and remember that like other sources of protein, chicken should be eaten in moderation.

Doultry

Asian-style barbecued chicken

Use your favourite cut of chicken for this popular barbecue dish. If you have time, marinate the meat for 2 to 6 hours. It is lovely served with a salad.

SERVES 2

½ teaspoon honey

¼ teaspoon chilli paste

½ tablespoon low-salt soy sauce

¼ teaspoon sesame oil

½ clove garlic, finely chopped

½ teaspoon grated ginger

juice of ¼ lemon

freshly ground black pepper

2 chicken thighs, skinned and trimmed of all visible fat

For the marinade, mix the honey with the chilli paste, soy sauce, sesame oil, garlic, ginger, lemon juice and a little black pepper in a medium-sized bowl.

Add the chicken and coat thoroughly with the marinade. Cover with foil and refrigerate until 10 minutes before cooking.

Heat a lightly oiled barbecue or grill and cook the chicken for about 15–20 minutes, turning several times during cooking. Avoid burning the chicken. Alternatively, you can cook the chicken in the oven at 180°C (350°F) for 25 minutes.

Chicken maryland & vegetables with a gherkin & mustard sauce

You can adapt this very French dish to your taste by changing the vegetables.

SERVES 2

1 large carrot, cut into sixths

2 sticks celery, peeled and quartered

4 medium mushrooms, halved

2 small chicken Maryland, skin and visible fat removed

salt and freshly ground black pepper

1 small leek, halved lengthwise and quartered

1 cup water

1 tablespoon chopped gherkins

1 tablespoon chopped parsley

1 spring onion, finely sliced

1 teaspoon Dijon mustard

In a large saucepan place the carrot, celery and mushrooms. Put the chicken on top, season with a little salt and pepper and top with the leeks. Pour over the water and bring to a simmer. Cover tightly with a lid and cook for about 25 minutes until the chicken is cooked.

Transfer the cooking liquid to a small saucepan. Bring to the boil and reduce the liquid by half. Stir in the gherkins, parsley, spring onion and mustard.

To serve, place the chicken and vegetables onto plates and spoon over the sauce.

Pan-fried chicken fillet with Madeira sauce & vegetables

This dish illustrates how to make a delicious and light low-fat sauce.
Trim off all chicken fat and skin and use a non-stick frying pan.

SERVES 2

1 medium carrot, peeled and
cut into small sticks

1 stick celery, peeled and cut
into small sticks

½ cup water

1 teaspoon olive oil

2 skinned chicken fillets

100 g (3½ oz) mushrooms, sliced

1 tablespoon dry Madeira

1 teaspoon cornflour mixed
with 1 tablespoon water

salt and freshly ground black pepper

1 tablespoon chopped parsley

Place the carrots and celery into a saucepan with the
water. Bring to the boil, cover with a tight-fitting lid and
cook on low heat for about 5 minutes or until the
vegetables are tender.

Heat the oil in a non-stick pan and brown the chicken
on one side for about 4 minutes. Turn the chicken, cover
with foil or a lid and cook for a further 5 minutes.
Transfer the chicken to plates and keep warm. Add
mushrooms to the pan and cook on high heat for 2
minutes. Add the Madeira, bring to the boil and add the
cooking juices from the vegetables. Return to the boil
and stir in the cornflour and water mixture to thicken the
sauce slightly. Season with salt, pepper and parsley.

To serve, place the vegetables around the chicken and
spoon over the sauce.

Chicken curry with vegetables

Cooking a curry is very pleasurable, especially when the spices release their exotic aroma into the kitchen. It is easier to make a curry in a wok in which the food can be easily mixed.

SERVES 4

½ brown onion

2 cm (¾ in) piece of ginger

2 cloves garlic

1 tablespoon peanut *or* canola oil

½ teaspoon fennel seeds

¼ teaspoon cummin seeds

2 teaspoons curry powder

3 tomatoes, chopped

4–6 skinless chicken pieces on the bone such as thighs or drumsticks

150 g (5 oz) mushrooms, sliced

2 cups cauliflower, divided into small florets

200 g (7 oz) baby spinach leaves

½ teaspoon hot chilli paste

Blend the onion, ginger and garlic to a fine purée. Alternatively, chop finely by hand.

Heat up a wok and add the oil. When the oil is hot, add the fennel seeds, cummin seeds and puréed onion, ginger and garlic. Cook on medium heat without browning for 3–4 minutes. Add the curry powder and stir well for about 30 seconds. Then add the tomatoes. Bring to a simmer, add the chicken pieces and stir well. Cover and simmer for 10 minutes.

Stir the curry well and add the mushrooms and cauliflower. Stir again. Cover and cook for a further 15 minutes.

Add the spinach, cover and cook until it has softened – this takes only a few minutes. Stir through the chilli paste and serve.

Stir-fried chicken with snowpeas & cloud ear mushrooms

Cloud ear mushroom or *wun yee* is a mushroom that is very popular with Chinese families.
It is now sold fresh in Asian foodstores, but the dried ones work just as well.

SERVES 4

about 2 tablespoons dried cloud ear
    mushrooms (*wun yee*)

400 g (14 oz) skinless chicken fillets or
    thigh meat, cut into ½ cm (about ¼ in)
    slices across the grain

1 teaspoon sugar

a pinch of salt

2 teaspoons cornflour

1 tablespoon shaoshing wine (Chinese
    rice wine) *or* dry sherry

2 tablespoons light soy sauce

1½ tablespoons peanut oil

400 g (14 oz) snowpeas, topped
    and tailed

3 thin slices fresh ginger

2 spring onions, cut into 1 cm (⅓ in) pieces

an extra 1 teaspoon cornflour mixed with
    2 tablespoons water

1 teaspoon sesame oil

Soak the mushrooms in a bowl of boiling water from the kettle. When almost cold, drain and rinse under cold water. Trim away any hard bits.

Toss the chicken strips into a bowl with the sugar, salt, cornflour, wine and half a tablespoon of the soy sauce.

Add half a tablespoon of the peanut oil to a hot wok and, when oil is hot, stir-fry the snowpeas and mushrooms on high heat for about 1 minute. If it starts to burn, add 1 tablespoon cold water. Transfer to a bowl.

Heat the remaining oil in the wok and stir in the ginger and spring onion. Add the marinated chicken and stir-fry on high heat for about 2 minutes. Stir in the cornflour mixed with water, remaining soy sauce and the sesame oil. Return the vegetables to the wok and toss well to combine the flavours. Serve immediately.

Mediterranean-style chicken casserole

Use skinless chicken pieces on the bone for this delicious dish.
You can prepare the dish one day in advance if you wish.

SERVES 3

1 tablespoon olive oil

3–6 skinless chicken pieces on the bone such as drumsticks or thighs

½ brown onion, chopped

2 sprigs of lemon thyme

1 green capsicum, seeded and cut into eighths

3 tomatoes, finely chopped

½ cup dry white wine

100 g (3½ oz) mushrooms, halved

6 pitted black olives (optional)

salt and freshly ground black pepper

1 clove garlic, finely chopped

1 tablespoon finely sliced basil

Heat the oil in a non-stick saucepan and, on medium heat, brown the chicken pieces for 1 minute on each side. Transfer to a plate.

Add onion and thyme to the pan and, on medium heat, stir-fry for 2 minutes. Add the capsicum and stir-fry for 2 minutes. Add the tomatoes and stir well before adding the wine, mushrooms, olives and chicken pieces.

Season with a little salt and pepper and bring to a simmer. Cover and cook for about 20 minutes.

Just before serving, stir in the garlic and basil.

Chicken couscous

Couscous is one of my all-time favourite dishes to share
with good friends. Here is a Tunisian version.

SERVES 6–8

6–12 chicken drumsticks, skinned

a handful of silverbeet leaves, shredded

3–4 sprigs of parsley

3 tablespoons tomato paste

1 tablespoon ground cummin

1 tablespoon harissa *or*
Asian-style chilli paste

3 tablespoons olive oil

6 medium carrots, peeled
and quartered

4 turnips, peeled and quartered

2 red or green capsicums, halved,
seeded and quartered

2 litres water *or* chicken stock (p. 204)

salt and freshly ground black pepper

1 ½ cups cooked chickpeas from a
can, drained

about 3 cups couscous

Place the drumsticks, silverbeet, parsley, tomato paste,
cummin, harissa, olive oil, carrots, turnips and capsicum
in a saucepan. Stir briefly to mix then add the stock and
season with salt and pepper. Bring to the boil, cover
and simmer for 30 minutes.

Add the cooked chickpeas and cook for a further
15 minutes.

Place the couscous in a fine strainer and run cold water
over it for a few minutes. Place a damp cloth or piece
of muslin in the perforated compartment of your
steamer. Place the wet couscous on the cloth and bring
the water in the steamer to the boil. Steam the
couscous, uncovered, for about 10 minutes until the
grains are soft.

Spoon the couscous onto a large platter and spoon
about one-quarter of the juices over it with some of the
vegetables. Serve the remaining vegetables, meat and
juices in a separate bowl.

chef's note

I recommend th
beginners try th
simple casserol
It's guaranteed
impress your di
party guests

Chicken in Red-wine sauce with carrots

I have modified this superb French classic to make it lighter and more digestible.
It is a very enjoyable dish to cook and can be prepared in advance.

SERVES 4

8 small chicken thighs, skinned or other chicken pieces on the bone

a little plain flour

about 1 tablespoon peanut oil

1 small brown onion, peeled and finely diced

1 stick celery, finely diced

1 rasher lean bacon, cut into small strips

12 small mushrooms

1 tablespoon brandy

3/4 cup red wine

1 cup chicken stock

1 clove garlic, crushed

1/2 cup Italian-style tomato sauce, bottled or home-made (p. 210)

1 small bay leaf

freshly ground black pepper

2 medium carrots, peeled and cut into bite-size pieces

about 1 cup shelled peas

1 tablespoon chopped parsley

Coat the chicken thighs with a little flour.

Heat two medium saucepans with half a tablespoon of oil in each. In one pan, fry the onion and celery for 3–4 minutes on medium heat. In the second pan, fry the bacon for 2 minutes. Transfer the bacon to a bowl. In the empty pan, brown the chicken thighs. Transfer the browned chicken to the pan containing the celery and onion. In the empty saucepan cook the mushrooms on high heat for about 5 minutes. Transfer the mushrooms to a bowl.

Add brandy to the pan and bring to the boil. Add the wine, stock and garlic, and return to the boil. Add the tomato sauce and when it comes to a simmer, pour this liquid over the chicken and stir well, adding the bay leaf and seasoning with a little pepper. Add carrots to the chicken, stir, cover and cook for about 25 minutes.

Stir in the peas and cook uncovered for a further 10 minutes. Then add the bacon, mushrooms and chopped parsley. Stir through and serve.

Rabbit casserole with prunes

Rabbit is one of the most flavoursome meats and you can now buy rabbit pieces from good poultry shops. This dish is simple to prepare but takes 1½ hours to cook.

SERVES 2

½ tablespoon peanut oil

2 rabbit hind legs

1 sprig of thyme, finely chopped

¼ brown onion, diced

1 teaspoon tomato paste

1 clove garlic, crushed

½ cup red wine

1 cup boiling water

10 prunes, pitted

salt and freshly ground black pepper

2 carrots, sliced

1 tablespoon chopped parsley

Heat the oil in a non-stick saucepan and brown the rabbit pieces. Add the thyme and onion, and stir for 1 minute before adding the tomato paste, garlic and wine. Bring to the boil, add the boiling water and prunes, and season with salt and pepper. Lower to a simmer, cover and cook for 1 hour.

After 1 hour, add the carrots, cover and cook for a further 30 minutes. Check that the rabbit is tender. Cook a little longer if necessary.

Stir in the parsley and serve.

Chicken Satay

If barbecuing these satays on bamboo sticks, soak the sticks for at least 20 minutes in cold water before use to prevent them from burning. You will need about 6 bamboo sticks. Serve with a choice of salads. Sambal oelek is readily available from Asian foodstores.

SERVES 2

juice of ¼ lemon

1 teaspoon soy sauce

1 teaspoon honey

½ clove garlic, finely chopped

¼ teaspoon turmeric (optional)

¼ teaspoon paprika

¼ teaspoon ground cummin

¼ teaspoon chilli paste (sambal oelek), or to taste

1 teaspoon peanut oil

a little freshly ground black pepper

250 g (9 oz) deboned, skinned chicken meat, cut into bite-sized pieces

2 lemon wedges or peanut sauce (p. 207)

To make the marinade, in a medium bowl combine the lemon juice, soy sauce, honey, garlic, turmeric, paprika, cummin, chilli paste, oil and pepper. Toss chicken in this marinade and refrigerate until required. Marinate the chicken for several hours but for no more than 6 hours.

Thread the meat onto skewers and cook under the grill. Alternatively, cook either in a frying pan brushed with a little oil, on a barbecue or on a rack in a hot oven. The satays will take only a few minutes to cook. Be careful not to overcook; the satays are much tastier moist than hard and dry.

Serve with lemon wedges or with peanut sauce.

Roast Christmas turkey

It is great fun cooking a large roast for a special occasion. All you need to remember
is to cook the turkey a little ahead of time and allow it to rest before carving.
The bread and orange stuffing, which can be made the day before, is delicious,
and keeps the meat moist during cooking. It can be omitted if you like.

SERVES 8–12

1 quantity of bread and orange stuffing (p. 155)

3.5 kg (about 7½ lb) turkey

2 tablespoons olive oil

4 sprigs of thyme, finely chopped

salt and freshly ground black pepper

1 large brown onion, cut into sixths

1 large carrot, diced

2 tablespoons brandy

1 cup dry white wine

2 cups water *or* chicken stock (p. 204)

2 teaspoons cornflour mixed with 2 tablespoons water

2 tablespoons chopped parsley *or* tarragon *or* basil

Preheat the oven to 150°C (300°F).

Place three-quarters of the stuffing inside the cleaned and emptied cavity of the turkey. Place the remaining stuffing in the wishbone cavity under the skin and neck. Truss the thighs with kitchen string to hold the stuffing inside.

Mix the olive oil with the thyme and a little salt and pepper and brush the turkey with it. Place the turkey on one side in your largest roasting tray on an oven rack. Roast the turkey in the preheated oven for about 45 minutes and turn to other side. Add the onion and carrot to the roasting tray and roast for a further 45 minutes. Turn the turkey onto its back, baste with the cooking juices and cook for a further 30–40 minutes. Pierce the thickest part of the turkey with a skewer to check if it's done – the juices should run clear.

Remove the turkey from the oven, place on a large serving dish, cover with foil and leave to rest for at least 15 minutes or until ready to serve.

Drain the fat from the roasting tray and place the tray on medium heat on top of the stove. Add the brandy and stir with the vegetables in the tray to extract as much flavour as possible. Add the wine and bring to the boil. Add the stock, raise the heat, and simmer for 5 minutes. Strain the sauce into a small saucepan. Discard the vegetables. Bring the sauce to the boil and whisk in the cornflour and water mixture. The sauce will thicken a little. Season with salt and pepper and stir in the parsley before serving.

Serve each person with a thin slice of turkey breast, a little stuffing and a small piece of leg meat. Spoon over a little gravy. Merry Christmas!

Bread & orange stuffing

I have enjoyed this stuffing ever since I was a little boy, when my
grandmother used to make it to stuff turkey, chicken, river fish and tomatoes.
This quantity is sufficient to stuff a 3.5 kg (about 7½ lb) turkey.

SERVES 10

600 g (1¼ lb) wholemeal bread,
   cut into small pieces

3 cups milk

1 tablespoon olive oil

1 large brown onion, finely chopped

2 cloves garlic, crushed

1 tablespoon finely grated orange rind

1 tablespoon butter *or* 1 tablespoon
   extra-virgin olive oil

2 tablespoons brandy

juice of ½ lemon

3 tablespoons chopped parsley
   or tarragon *or* basil

salt and freshly ground black pepper

Place the bread in a bowl. Bring the milk to the boil and
pour over the bread. Allow to soak.

Heat the oil in a non-stick saucepan and over medium
heat stir-fry the onion for about 5 minutes or until soft.
Add the garlic, stir for 1 minute, then stir in the orange
rind. Add the bread and milk preparation, lower the
heat and mix until a sticky paste forms. Mix in the butter,
brandy, lemon juice and parsley. Season with salt and
pepper and remove from the heat.

You can use the stuffing immediately or allow to cool
and refrigerate. Use within 1 day.

Most of us love the flavour of beef, lamb and pork, and in recent times butchers have dramatically changed the way they cut and present meat. The cuts on offer now are smaller and leaner than they were ten years ago. A moderate serve of lean meat of around 125 to 150 g (4 to 5 oz) per person, cooked in a minimum of fat and served with plenty of vegetables makes a good occasional meal. In the context of this book, which aims to reduce the risk of cancers related to what we eat, try to avoid eating beef and lamb fat, burning the meat during cooking, browning it too much or overcooking. Take care especially when you cook on the barbecue. Make sure your barbecue is very clean and preheat it well before starting. Don't cook over an open flame and avoid squeezing the juices out of the meat and moving the meat around as it cooks. Serve the meat as soon as it is cooked.

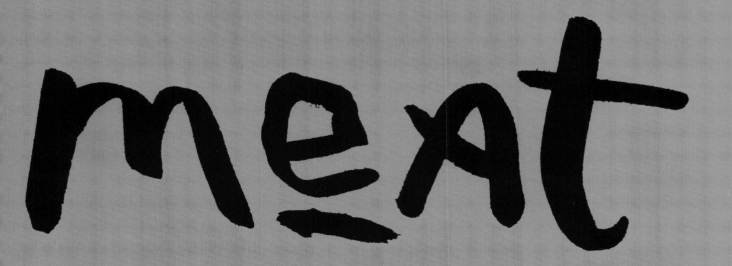

meat

Pan-fried or grilled steak

This is the basic method of cooking a steak. Buy a piece of steak about 2.5 cm (1 in) thick and weighing no more than 150 g (5 oz) per person. Buy the steak on the day you cook it and avoid keeping for more than 2 days. If you are unsure about the freshness, just smell it. Any off smell indicates it's no longer fresh.

SERVES 1

about 1 teaspoon peanut,
  canola or olive oil

150 g (5 oz) steak, trimmed

a little salt (optional)

freshly ground black pepper

Brush a grill or non-stick pan with oil and place on medium heat for about 1 minute. Place the steak on the grill or pan. Avoid moving or poking the steak during cooking.

If you like your steak medium-rare, turn after 3 minutes and cook the other side for a further 2–3 minutes. If you prefer your steak well-done, cook it for 5 minutes on one side before turning it over and cooking for a further 4–5 minutes. Avoid burning the steak, and increase or decrease the heat as you feel necessary. When the steak is cooked, transfer to a plate, season with salt and pepper and serve.

Steak with tomato & olive sauce

If you have no Italian-style tomato sauce, use half a can of peeled, chopped tomatoes. Some of the sauce ingredients are quite salty so no added salt is necessary. Serve with steamed vegetables.

SERVES 2

½ tablespoon olive oil

2 x 150 g (5 oz) lean steaks such as rump,
  porterhouse or fillet

1 clove garlic, chopped

1 anchovy fillet, chopped (optional)

4 capers, chopped

½ cup Italian-style tomato sauce, bottled
  or home-made (p. 210)

6 black olives, pitted

1 tablespoon chopped parsley or finely
  sliced basil

freshly ground black pepper

Heat the olive oil in a non-stick frying pan and on medium heat cook the steaks for 3–5 minutes on each side. Refer to the instructions for pan-fried steak for approximate cooking times. When the steaks are cooked to your liking, transfer to a serving dish and cover with foil.

With the pan on low heat add the garlic, anchovy and capers and fry for 30 seconds. Stir in the tomato sauce and olives, increase the heat, and bring to the boil. Add the parsley and season with pepper. Serve the sauce on or around the steaks.

Stir-fried beef with ginger & chinese cabbage

You can use any vegetable in this popular dish but I find that
Chinese cabbage works really well, since it absorbs the flavourings nicely.

SERVES 2

½ tablespoon shaoshing wine (Chinese rice wine) or dry sherry

1 teaspoon cornflour

freshly ground black pepper

½ tablespoon cold water

200 g (7 oz) very lean beef such as skirt or rump

1 tablespoon peanut oil

about 200 g (7 oz) Chinese cabbage, finely shredded

1 clove garlic, finely sliced

2 teaspoons grated ginger

½ tablespoon low-salt soy sauce

½ teaspoon sesame oil

To make the marinade, combine the rice wine with the cornflour, pepper and cold water in a medium bowl.

Cut the beef into ½ cm (¼ in) slices across the grain. Place in the marinade and allow to sit for at least 10 minutes.

Pour a third of the peanut oil into a hot wok and stir-fry the cabbage for about 5 minutes or until soft. If it starts burning, pour 1 tablespoon of water down the side of the wok. Transfer the cabbage to a bowl.

Heat the remaining oil in the wok and stir in the garlic and ginger. Add the beef and stir-fry on high heat for about 20–30 seconds until it changes colour. Stir in the soy sauce, return the cabbage to the pan and toss to mix through. Just before serving, stir in the sesame oil.

chef's note

The meatballs
are also delicio
served with pol
and pan-fried
zucchinis.

Meatballs with sauce

This lovely dish can be served with pasta, noodles, rice, steamed potatoes or polenta.
Buy the minced beef on the day you make the dish or no earlier than one day before.
If you wish, you can use chicken, veal or pork mince instead.

SERVES 4

400 g (14 oz) lean ground beef

3 tablespoons breadcrumbs

2 tablespoons cold water

2 cloves garlic, chopped

2 tablespoons chopped parsley

1 tablespoon finely sliced basil

1 egg

salt and freshly ground black pepper

a little plain flour

1 tablespoon olive oil

2 tablespoons dry white *or* red wine
   or 2 teaspoons brandy

about 2 cups Italian-style tomato sauce,
   bottled or home-made (p. 210)

1 teaspoon finely grated or
   chopped orange rind

In a bowl, and using your hands, thoroughly combine the ground beef with the breadcrumbs, water, half the garlic, half the parsley, half the basil and egg. Season and combine a little more.

Form the mince into small balls about the size of golf balls, dipping your hands in water after each one. Coat each ball lightly with flour.

Heat the oil in a wide, non-stick frying pan and on medium heat brown the meatballs for about 1 minute on each side. Add the wine to the pan and bring to the boil. Add the tomato sauce and orange rind, bring to a simmer and cook for about 8 minutes, stirring the meatballs occasionally and spooning over the sauce to keep them moist. Stir in the remaining garlic, parsley and basil, season with black pepper and serve.

Mexican-style meatloaf

This meatloaf has the Mexican flavours of cummin and chilli. It can be enjoyed
with an Italian-style tomato sauce and I like to serve it with mashed potatoes and a green salad.
You need a greased loaf tin.

SERVES 8

1 tablespoon olive oil

1/4 teaspoon cummin seeds

1 cup finely diced carrots

about 1/2 cup finely diced
red capsicum

about 1 cup finely diced
eggplant

1/2 cup shelled peas

1/2 teaspoon ground cummin

1/2 cup water

800 g (1 3/4 lb) ground lean beef

1/2 cup fresh breadcrumbs

1/2 teaspoon hot chilli paste

a little salt and freshly ground
black pepper

1 tablespoon tomato ketchup

Heat the oil in a large non-stick frying pan and gently
stir-fry the cummin seeds, carrots and capsicum for
1 minute. Add the eggplant, peas and ground cummin,
stir and cook for 2 minutes. Add half the water and
cook for a further 2 minutes. Allow to cool a little.

Preheat the oven to 220°C (450°F).

Mix the ground beef with the breadcrumbs, cooked
vegetables, remaining water, chilli paste and a little
salt and pepper. Mix thoroughly for about 1 minute,
spoon the preparation into a greased loaf tin and
brush the top with ketchup. Bake in a preheated
oven for 20 minutes, then lower the temperature to
180°C (350°F) and cook for a further 20 minutes.

Remove the meatloaf from the oven and leave to rest
for 10 minutes before carefully slicing with a serrated
knife.

Steak & kidney casserole with carrots

This dish, a modern version of a popular classic, practically cooks itself and is delicious served with plenty of carrots. To keep the dish healthy, it is important to trim the meat of all fat. It takes about 2 hours to cook.

SERVES 2

about 150 g (5 oz) lean casserole beef, trimmed and cubed

about 150 g (5 oz) lean beef kidney, trimmed and cubed

½ tablespoon plain flour

salt and freshly ground black pepper

½ tablespoon peanut or canola oil

½ brown onion, finely diced

2 sprigs of parsley, roughly chopped

½ cup Italian-style tomato sauce, bottled or home-made (p. 210)

3 tablespoons red wine

½ cup water

1 clove garlic, crushed

2 large carrots, cut into bite-size pieces

Mix the beef and kidney with the flour, a little salt and black pepper.

Preheat the oven to 180°C (350°F).

Heat the oil in an ovenproof casserole dish and gently fry the onion for about 5 minutes. Switch off the heat and add the beef, kidney and parsley. Add the tomato sauce, wine, water and garlic without stirring. Place the carrots on top. Do not stir them in. Cover the pan with a layer of foil then with a lid. Cook in the preheated oven for about 2 hours.

Stir the beef, kidney and vegetables together just before serving. This dish is lovely with mashed potato.

This is a dish for
the more confid
cook.

Roast beef fillet with sweet vegetables

Although beef fillet is one of the dearest cuts of meat, there is little wastage. Here, the beef is stuffed with cooked vegetables.

SERVES 3

½ tablespoon olive oil

¼ teaspoon cummin seeds

½ brown onion, diced

about 300 g (11 oz) pumpkin flesh, cut into 1 cm (⅓ in) dice

about 300 g (11 oz) sweet potatoes, cut into 1 cm (⅓ in) dice

½ cup Italian-style tomato sauce, bottled or home-made (p. 210)

½ cup water

salt and freshly ground black pepper

a pinch of cayenne pepper

2 tablespoons chopped parsley

about 250 g (9 oz) peas, cooked and drained

450 g (almost 1 lb) piece of beef fillet

1 small carrot, diced

½ cup water

½ cup dry white wine

1 teaspoon cornflour mixed with 1 tablespoon water

Heat half the oil in a medium-sized pan. Stir in the cummin seeds and half of the onions and fry for 2 minutes. Add the pumpkin, sweet potatoes, tomato sauce and water. Cover and cook until the vegetables are tender. Drain the vegetables, reserving the juices. Season with a little salt, cayenne, black pepper and chopped parsley. Stir in the cooked peas. Cool.

Preheat the oven to 200°C (400°F).

Using a small, sharp knife and starting at the smaller end of the fillet, make a little cut into the meat but don't slit right through to the other end. Fill this pocket with some of the vegetables.

Brush a small, heavy roasting tray with the remaining oil and, over high heat, brown the beef on all sides. Add the onion mixture and bake in the preheated oven for 15–20 minutes. Transfer to a warm serving platter, cover with foil and rest for about 10 minutes.

Place the roasting tray on medium heat and stir-fry the rest of the onion and carrot for 1 minute. Add the white wine, reserved vegetable juices and ½ cup water. Boil for 2–3 minutes then strain this into a small saucepan. Return to the boil and stir in the cornflour preparation. Season to taste.

Cut the beef into 3 slices. Spoon a little sauce onto each plate and top each with a slice of beef. Season with extra pepper and serve with the leftover vegetables.

Veal or Beef osso buco

This classic Italian dish, superb in winter, can be made with either veal or beef. Using veal will produce a more delicate dish than beef; it is, however, more expensive. Beef will also take about an hour longer to cook. Whichever you use, be sure to trim all visible fat from the meat. I suggest cooking the dish in a large saucepan or in an ovenproof dish.

SERVES 4

2 tablespoons olive oil

½ brown onion, finely chopped

1 medium carrot, finely chopped

1 stick celery, finely chopped

4–8 slices shin of veal *or* beef, cut into 3 cm (1½ in) slices

a little plain flour

½ cup dry white wine

1 cup beef *or* veal stock (p. 205)

400 g (14 oz) can peeled tomatoes, chopped

1 teaspoon tomato paste

2 sprigs of thyme

1 clove garlic, crushed

salt and freshly ground black pepper

rind of ½ lemon, finely grated

2 tablespoons chopped parsley

Heat half the oil in a wide saucepan and cook the onion, carrot and celery for about 5 minutes. Transfer to a plate.

Lightly coat the veal or beef slices with flour. Heat the remaining oil in the pan and brown the meat on both sides for about 2 minutes on each side. Add the wine, stock, tomatoes, tomato paste, thyme and garlic to the pan. Season with a little salt and pepper and gently stir in the cooked onion, carrot and celery. Bring to a simmer, cover the pan and cook for about 1½ hours if you're using veal, and 2–2½ hours for beef. It can also be cooked in a preheated oven at 150°C (300°F) for about the same duration.

Just before serving, stir in the lemon rind and chopped parsley.

Veal fillet with carrots & Fines Herbs

Veal fillet is lean, delicate and tender. European butchers usually specialise in quality veal, but it is always wise to order it in advance. Don't worry if you can't get all the herbs, but you must try it at least once with tarragon.

SERVES 4

600 g (1 ¼ lb) baby carrots, peeled and cut into bite-size pieces

½ cup water

1 teaspoon peanut oil

about 600 g (1 ¼ lb) veal fillet, cut into 3 cm (1 ½ in) slices

salt and freshly ground black pepper

2 tablespoons port

1 cup veal (p. 205) or vegetable stock (p. 203)

1 teaspoon cornflour mixed with 2 tablespoons water

1 tablespoon finely chopped tarragon

1 tablespoon finely chopped parsley

about 18 small sprigs of chervil

Place the carrots in a saucepan with half a cup of water. Cover and cook until soft.

Heat the oil in a non-stick pan and cook the veal slices on both sides until just done. Each side takes about 3–4 minutes. Transfer the veal to a warm plate, season with a little salt and pepper, and keep warm under foil or a lid.

Add port to the pan and allow to reduce a little before adding the stock and all of the carrot cooking juices. Return to the boil and reduce the liquid to about 1 cup. Stir in the cornflour mixture and bring to a simmer. Toss the carrots in the sauce with the herbs and season.

Place the veal on plates with the carrots and spoon over the sauce. Garnish with sprigs of chervil and serve.

Lamb cutlets with thyme & tomatoes

Select very lean lamb cutlets and, if there are
none on display, ask your butcher to cut some up for you.
This dish is lovely with mashed potatoes.

SERVES 1

2 tomatoes, diced

½ tablespoon olive oil

½ clove garlic, finely chopped

1 sprig of thyme, finely chopped

3 lean lamb cutlets, trimmed

salt and freshly ground black pepper

juice of ¼ lemon

Mix the tomato with half of the oil, the garlic and half of the thyme.

Sprinkle cutlets with the remaining thyme. Heat the remaining oil in a non-stick frying pan and cook the cutlets for 3 minutes on one side. Turn, and cook for about 2 minutes on the other. Transfer to a plate and season with salt and pepper.

Add the tomato mixture to the pan, increase the heat and stir for 1 minute. Spoon over the meat and serve sprinkled with lemon juice.

Lamb steak with zucchini & Roast pumpkin

With the new cuts of lamb available,
butchers now sell lean lamb steaks taken from the leg.
Serve with a green salad or a green vegetable.

SERVES 2

about 1 tablespoon olive oil

½ clove garlic, finely chopped

1 teaspoon chopped rosemary
   or thyme

2 x 150 g (5 oz) lamb steaks,
   trimmed of fat

about 250 g (9 oz) butternut pumpkin
   or other pumpkin of your choice,
   skin on, cut into 1 cm (⅓ in) slices

¼ teaspoon sweet paprika

salt and freshly ground black pepper

2 zucchinis, cut diagonally into
   ½ cm (¼ in) slices

juice of ¼ lemon

Preheat the oven to 220°C (450°F).

Combine half the oil, the garlic and the rosemary in a bowl and brush the lamb steaks with this marinade. Leave to marinate while you prepare the vegetables.

Place the pumpkin on an oven tray lined with baking paper (optional) and brush the pumpkin lightly with a little oil seasoned with paprika and pepper. Bake in the preheated oven for about 20 minutes, turning over halfway through.

Five minutes before the pumpkin is ready, brush a non-stick pan or grill with the remaining olive oil and cook the lamb for about 3 minutes on medium heat. Turn the meat and cook the other side for a further 3 minutes. Remove from the pan and place in the oven with the pumpkin.

Add the zucchini to the pan or grill and cook on each side for about 1 minute. Serve the pumpkin on plates topped with meat. Season to taste, and top with the zucchini. Drizzle over the lemon juice and serve.

Grilled loin of lamb provençale

This dish was inspired by a visit to the south of France. For the presentation
of the dish I used a piece of PVC pipe of about 10 cm (4 in) in diameter
and 5 cm (2 in) high to arrange the vegetables and meat neatly. Alternatively,
you can use a round pastry cutter about 10 cm (4 in) in diameter.
I usually cook the meat on a cast-iron grill but it can be cooked in a pan.

SERVES 2

2 deboned racks of lamb, each containing 4 chops, trimmed

2 sprigs of lemon thyme, finely chopped

3 teaspoons olive oil

salt and freshly ground black pepper

1 tomato, diced

a few basil leaves, finely sliced

1 clove garlic, finely chopped

½ red capsicum, sliced

150 g (5 oz) mushrooms, sliced

about 100 g (3½ oz) baby spinach leaves

a pinch of cayenne pepper

Season the meat with half the lemon thyme, 1 teaspoon oil and a little pepper.

Mix the tomato in a bowl with 1 teaspoon of oil, the remaining lemon thyme, basil and garlic.

Heat the remaining oil in a non-stick pan and on low heat stir-fry the capsicum for 1 minute. Add the mushrooms, increase the heat and stir-fry for 1 minute. Add the spinach and stir until wilted. Season with salt, pepper and cayenne pepper.

Preheat the grill to medium and, when hot, cook the lamb for about 4 minutes on each side. Season with pepper, and leave to rest for 3 or 4 minutes before serving. Slice the meat if you wish.

To serve, place the PVC rings (or pastry cutters) on plates and spoon the vegetables into the rings. Top with the meat and lift off. Spoon the tomato sauce around and serve.

Loin of lamb with Green flageolet beans

Green flageolet beans are one of the most delicious beans. Few people grow them in Australia but you can get the canned variety in gourmet shops and delis. The French love to serve lamb and flageolet beans together, along with a green salad.

SERVES 6

900 g (almost 2 lb) loin of lamb, trimmed

2 tablespoons olive oil

1 tablespoon chopped rosemary

salt and freshly ground black pepper

about 300 g (11 oz) pumpkin, cut into 1 cm (1/3 in) slices

1 small carrot, diced

1 small onion, diced

about 300 g (11 oz) French beans

400 g (14 oz) can green flageolet beans

1 teaspoon tomato paste

1/4 cup red wine

1 clove garlic, crushed

1 cup beef stock (p. 205)

Preheat the oven to 200°C (400°F).

Coat the lamb with half of the oil and the rosemary and season with pepper.

Heat the remaining oil in a roasting tray and brown the meat and pumpkin pieces for a few minutes on high heat. Add the carrot and onion, place in the preheated oven and roast for 15 minutes.

Steam or microwave the French beans and reheat the flageolet beans in their juices.

Transfer the meat and pumpkin to a plate, season with salt and cover.

Place the roasting tray on medium heat, and stir the tomato paste into the remaining vegetables in the roasting tray. Stir in the wine and garlic. Bring to the boil. Add the stock and boil for 2 minutes before straining the sauce into a small saucepan.

To serve, pour a little sauce onto hot plates and top with the sliced meat, vegetables and beans.

Roast leg of lamb with gravy

Many men I spoke to have nominated this as their favourite meal. It is best to trim the
meat of as much fat as possible and to avoid overcooking the meat so as to keep it tender.
Serve with roast vegetables and a steamed green vegetable or a salad.
Roast the vegetables in a separate oven tray.

SERVES 8

1.5 kg (3 lb) leg of lamb, trimmed

2 cloves garlic, peeled and quartered

2 tablespoons olive oil

¼ teaspoon chilli paste (optional)

1 tablespoon finely chopped thyme

salt and freshly ground black pepper

1 carrot, coarsely diced

1 onion, coarsely diced

1 teaspoon tomato paste

½ cup dry white wine

1 cup water

2 teaspoons cornflour mixed with
   1 tablespoon white wine

1 tablespoon chopped parsley

Preheat the oven to 180°C (350°F).

Using the tip of a small blade, make eight small cuts into
the lamb at regular intervals, ensuring that the cuts are
deep enough for the garlic slivers. The garlic must not
protrude from the meat.

Mix the olive oil with the chilli paste and thyme, and
brush the lamb all over with the mixture. Season with
black pepper, and place on a rack and sit in a roasting
tray. Roast the lamb for about 50 minutes, turning it two
or three times during cooking so that it cooks evenly.

Twenty minutes after the start of the cooking, add the
diced carrot and onion to the tray.

When the meat is done, remove from the oven. Place
on a dish, cover with foil and leave to rest for about
10 minutes before serving.

To make your gravy, drain as much fat as possible
from the tray. Keep the onions and carrots in the tray.
Place on medium heat and stir in the tomato paste.
Add the wine and boil to reduce the juices by half. Add
the water, bring to the boil and whisk in the cornflour
mixture. Add any meat juices from the plate and season
the gravy with salt and pepper. Strain into a small
saucepan and keep warm. Discard the carrots, onions
and herbs. Slice the meat and serve with the gravy
and parsley.

chef's note

Plan ahead and
cook the vegetal
in advance to cu
down on the las
minute preparat

Couscous with Grilled lamb kebabs

Couscous is a coarse wheat semolina, very popular in North African countries and in the south of Italy. The cooking instructions on the pack usually suggest cooking couscous in hot water but I find that steaming gives a lighter result. You will need to soak 2 bamboo skewers in cold water for about 30 minutes before using.

SERVES 2

250 g (9 oz) lean lamb meat
  from the leg, cubed

1 tablespoon olive oil

1 teaspoon ground cummin

1 clove garlic, finely chopped

1 teaspoon harissa *or* Asian-style
  chilli paste (sambal oelek)

salt and freshly ground black pepper

1 long carrot, peeled and quartered

1 turnip, peeled and quartered

1/2 red capsicum, seeded and quartered

1 zucchini, halved

2 tomatoes, quartered

1/2 tablespoon tomato paste

2 cups water

1/2 cup cooked chickpeas, drained

150 g (5 oz) couscous

a few sprigs of fresh coriander (garnish)

Place the lamb cubes in a bowl and mix with half the oil, half the cummin, half the garlic, half the harissa and a little pepper.

To a large saucepan add the carrot, turnip, capsicum, zucchini, tomatoes, tomato paste, water and the remaining oil, cummin, garlic and harissa. Season and bring to the boil. Lower to a simmer and cook for 15 minutes.

Add the drained chickpeas and cook for a further 10 minutes.

To prepare the couscous, place the couscous in a fine strainer and run cold water over it for a few minutes. Place a damp cloth or piece of muslin over the perforated compartment of your steamer. Place the damp couscous in the steamer on top of the cloth and bring the water in the steamer to the boil. Steam the couscous, uncovered, for about 10 minutes until the grains are soft.

Preheat the grill. Thread the lamb cubes onto skewers. Place the meat on the grill for about 8 minutes, turning the kebabs twice during the cooking.

Place the couscous in a serving dish with the kebabs on top. Garnish with the coriander. Serve the vegetables and juices in a bowl from the centre of the table for all to help themselves.

Stir-fried vegetables with Roast pork

You may have seen displayed in the windows of many Chinese restaurants
or take-aways the appetising red-coloured roasted strips of lean pork.
These are sold by weight, and you can ask for them to be sliced or left whole.
Ask for a whole piece, unsliced, for this recipe.

SERVES 2

½ tablespoon peanut *or* canola oil

¼ teaspoon sesame oil

1 teaspoon grated ginger

1 clove garlic, sliced

about 100 g (3½ oz) cabbage,
   finely sliced

100 g (3½ oz) sugar peas *or*
   snowpeas, topped and tailed

100 g (3½ oz) mushrooms of
   your choice, finely sliced

8 baby corn cobs from a can, drained

about 250 g (9 oz) Chinese roast
   pork, sliced diagonally into
   bite-size pieces

½ tablespoon low-salt soy sauce

¼ teaspoon chilli paste

2 spring onions, finely sliced

a few sprigs of fresh coriander

Heat the wok and add the peanut and sesame oils.
Stir in the ginger and garlic and immediately add
the cabbage. Stir-fry for 30 seconds. Add about
1 tablespoon cold water down the side of the wok if
the cabbage starts sticking or burning. Add the sugar
peas and stir-fry for 30 seconds. Then add the
mushrooms and baby corn, and stir-fry until the
vegetables are soft.

Stir in the pork, soy sauce and chilli paste, and stir to
distribute the flavours and heat through. If you wish,
you could reheat the pork in the oven and serve it on
top of the stir-fried vegetables. Serve sprinkled with
spring onion and coriander leaves.

Lamb shanks with vegetables

This great winter classic is full of flavour and texture. It is best cooked in an ovenproof casserole and takes about 2 hours. If you are short of time, cook it in a pressure cooker, in which case reduce the cooking time to around 40 minutes. As the dish is rich, select small shanks.

SERVES 4

1 tablespoon olive oil

4 lamb shanks, trimmed of all visible fat

3 sprigs of thyme

½ brown onion, chopped

1 tablespoon red wine vinegar or ½ cup dry white wine

1½ cups Italian-style tomato sauce, bottled or home-made (p. 210)

1 cup water

1 clove garlic, crushed

8 baby carrots, peeled and left whole

2 sticks celery, cut into 5 cm (2 in) pieces

1 red capsicum, halved and cut into eighths

salt and freshly ground black pepper

Preheat the oven to 150°C (300°F).

Heat the oil in a large casserole dish and brown the shanks for a few minutes. Add the thyme and onion, and stir for 2 minutes. Add the vinegar, tomato sauce and water, and shake the pan a little before adding the garlic, whole carrots, celery and capsicum.

Season with a little salt and pepper and stir well. Bring to a simmer, cover and cook in the preheated oven for about 2 hours or until the meat comes away from the bone.

Serve with boiled potatoes.

Stir-fried pork with shredded vegetables

For this quick dish, I use pork fillet, but you can also use pork loin or a cut that butchers sell as pork steak. When shredding the vegetables, cut them into long thin strips, about the size of the bean sprouts.

SERVES 2

1 tablespoon peanut *or* canola oil

2 teaspoons grated ginger

about 100 g (3½ oz) Chinese cabbage (*wong nga bak*)

about 100 g (3½ oz) bean sprouts

1 stick tender celery, cut into 6 cm (2 in) strips

2 mushrooms, finely sliced

1 medium carrot, cut into 6 cm (2 in) strips

1 clove garlic, finely sliced

200 g (7 oz) pork fillet or very lean pork, sliced

½ tablespoon low-salt soy sauce

½ teaspoon sesame oil

¼ teaspoon chilli paste (optional)

a few sprigs of fresh coriander

Heat a wok and, when hot, add a third of the oil. Add the ginger, cabbage, bean sprouts, celery, mushroom and carrot and stir-fry until soft. If the mixture starts to burn or stick to the pan, add 2 tablespoons water down the side of the wok. Transfer the vegetables to a plate.

Heat the remaining oil in the wok. Add the garlic and pork, and stir-fry until the pork changes colour. Stir in the soy sauce, sesame oil and chilli. Return the vegetables to the pan and reheat well. Serve garnished with coriander leaves.

Desserts

Rich desserts containing lots of cream, butter and chocolate are a nice treat for special occasions. On a daily basis, however, desserts can be seen as a way to complement the rest of the day's diet. So treat yourself to delicious seasonal fruits by eating grapes in autumn, oranges in winter, strawberries in spring and summer, and so on. For more special treats, learn to make luscious fruit salads – there are a few lovely ones in this chapter. During winter, fruits can also be stewed and eaten over a few days. And remember that dried fruits such as figs and apricots, and nuts such as walnuts and almonds make delightful desserts.

Low-fat dairy products such as yoghurt and cottage cheese are a good source of calcium. Low-fat puddings and slices are a nice way to finish a meal, as are pancakes. If you must have cream or ice-cream, be moderate in your servings.

Sweet creamy topping

This is a delicious alternative to cream and ice-cream. Serve with fruit salads or fruit desserts. I use a fresh low-fat cream cheese with a fat content of less than 8 per cent. Manufacturers call this cheese either smooth creamed cottage cheese, quark or fromage blanc.

SERVES 4

4 tablespoons fresh smooth creamed cottage cheese

3 tablespoons low-fat milk

½ tablespoon castor sugar *or* honey

1 teaspoon finely grated lemon *or* orange rind *or* a pinch of ground cinnamon *or* 2 drops pure vanilla essence

Whisk or blend all the ingredients to a creamy consistency and refrigerate until required.

Dates & orange on yoghurt

Oranges with dates and yoghurt are a refreshing and nourishing way to finish a meal.

SERVES 6–8

1 kg tub skim-milk natural yoghurt

2 tablespoons milk

2 tablespoons orange marmalade

2 tablespoons chopped almonds

1 orange, sliced or segmented

8–16 dates

Place the yoghurt, milk and marmalade in a bowl and whip together until smooth. Pour into a large dish. Sprinkle with almonds and top with orange slices and dates. Refrigerate until required.

Williams pears & passionfruit salad

For this easy, light, luscious dessert select Williams pears that are just ripe,
that is, light green turning yellow. You can make the salad several hours in advance
but make sure the liquid covers or coats the pears.

SERVES 4–6

4 oranges or 1 ½ cups best-quality
orange juice

juice of ½ lemon

3 heavy passionfruit

2 tablespoons sugar *or* orange
blossom honey (optional)

4 just-ripe Williams pears

1 tablespoon kirsch *or* Drambuie *or*
brandy (optional)

Squeeze the oranges into a bowl. Mix in the lemon
juice, passionfruit pulp and sugar or honey.

Peel, quarter and core the pears. Cut each quarter into
3 segments and add to the juices. Cover the bowl with
plastic film and refrigerate.

Remove from the refrigerator 15 minutes before serving.
Stir in the liqueur of your choice and serve.

Fresh fruit platter with two berry sauces

You can serve a seasonal fruit platter at any time of the year. My favourite
time is the warmer months of the year when the berries are sweet and delicious.
In this recipe I serve the fruits with a blueberry and raspberry sauce.

SERVES 4

200 g (7 oz) punnet blueberries

200 g (7 oz) punnet raspberries

juice of 2 oranges

juice of 1 lemon

2 tablespoons sugar

a selection of seasonal fruits for the
   platter: 4 apricots, 1 large peach,
   1 large bunch of grapes, 1 mango,
   ½ pawpaw, 250 g (9 oz) berries

In a blender purée the blueberries and a quarter of
the raspberries with half the orange juice, half the
lemon juice and half the sugar. Strain the sauce into
a bowl and refrigerate until 5 minutes before serving.

Blend the remaining raspberries with the remaining
orange and lemon juices and sugar. Strain into a bowl
and refrigerate until 5 minutes before serving.

Prepare the fruits for the platter by washing, peeling
and slicing as necessary. Pile the fruits attractively on
a platter and accompany with the two berry sauces.

chef's note

Take time when
choosing pawpa
Make sure it is
just ripe and
unblemished. If
not sure, ask you
greengrocer for

Peach, mango & berry fruit salad in pawpaw

These fabulous fruits are available to us at the end of summer and
what a treat they are! You can easily adapt the recipe according to the
availability of the fruits and use, say, pears instead of peaches or mangoes.
This salad makes an ideal finish to a summer Christmas lunch or dinner.

SERVES 4

juice of 2 oranges

juice of ½ lemon

1 tablespoon castor sugar

200 g (7 oz) punnet raspberries

3 peaches

1 medium mango

8 large strawberries

2 small pawpaws

Blend the orange and lemon juices, sugar and two-thirds of the raspberries to a purée. Strain into a serving bowl.

Wash the peaches and cut each into 8–12 segments. Peel the mango and cut into small pieces. Wash and slice the strawberries. Add all the fruits to the bowl with remaining whole raspberries. Stir gently and refrigerate.

Remove the salad from the refrigerator about 15 minutes before required. Just before serving, halve and peel the pawpaws and, with a spoon, scoop out the seeds. Spoon the fruit salad into the pawpaws and serve.

Baked Rhubarb & apple with grapefruit

This dessert is delicious hot or cold. To present it attractively, I sometimes use a piece of PVC pipe of 10 cm (4 in) in diameter and 5 cm (2 in) high. You can also use a round pastry cutter about 10 cm (4 in) in diameter, or just serve the fruits in individual soufflé bowls.

SERVES 2

2 Golden Delicious apples, peeled, halved, cored and cut into eighths

4 stalks rhubarb, peeled and cut into 4 cm (1¾ in) pieces

1½ tablespoons castor sugar

2 tablespoons water

2 grapefruit

Preheat the oven to 180°C (350°F).

In a bowl, gently toss together the apple, rhubarb and sugar. Place in a roasting tray with the water and bake in a preheated oven until just soft. This takes 15–20 minutes.

Peel the grapefruit, taking care to remove all the pith. Cut the grapefruit into segments, collecting any juice that results. To cut segments, use a small, sharp knife and insert the blade into the grapefruit along the fine skin which separates the sections. Turn the blade and come up the other side of the skin to release the fruit segment from its casing.

Place the PVC ring or pastry cutter on the plate. Spoon half the apple and rhubarb into the ring and top with grapefruit segments. Spoon over the cooking juices from the rhubarb and apple, and any grapefruit juice. Carefully lift off the ring before serving.

chef's note

The better the w[ine]
you use, the nice[r]
the smell in the
kitchen when you
prepare this
delicious dish.

Stewed figs & plums in red wine

Here is a luscious autumn weekend dessert. The dish is lovely either hot
or cold but I prefer it cold as the spices have released more of their flavour.

SERVES 4–6

½ bottle (375 ml) good red wine

½ cup water

3 tablespoons castor sugar

¼ vanilla pod, cut open lengthwise

2 cm (1 in) piece cinnamon stick

½ star anise

6 just-ripe blood plums, left whole

8 just-ripe black figs, left whole

Place the red wine, water, sugar, vanilla pod,
cinnamon and star anise in a medium saucepan.
Bring to the boil and simmer for 10 minutes.

Add the washed plums and figs to the pan, return
to a simmer and cook for about 10 minutes.

Gently place the fruit in a bowl and pour over the
liquid. If you wish the juice to have a stronger flavour,
boil it to reduce the juice by half before pouring over
the fruits.

Allow to cool before serving. If not using immediately,
refrigerate and remove from the refrigerator
20 minutes before serving.

Caramelised red plums with berries

This is a truly luscious dish with a magnificent ruby-red colour.
For presentation, sprinkle icing sugar on top just before serving.

SERVES 6

½ vanilla pod

4 tablespoons castor sugar

200 g (7 oz) punnet raspberries

200 g (7 oz) punnet blueberries

juice of 1 orange

juice of ½ lemon

6–12 red plums, halved and stoned

200 g (7 oz) punnet blackberries

a little icing sugar from a shaker

Split the vanilla pod in half and, using the blade of a small knife, scrape out the tiny black seeds. Mix these seeds with the sugar.

In a food processor blend half of the raspberries, one-third of the blueberries, the orange juice, lemon juice and half of the vanilla sugar to a purée. Strain this berry sauce into a jug.

Sprinkle the remaining sugar over the cut plums and place under a hot grill until the sugar starts to bubble.

Pour a little berry sauce into the centre of each plate. Place 2–4 plum halves on the sauce and arrange the blackberries and the remaining fruits around. Sprinkle with a little icing sugar and serve.

Pear & Prune loaf

There is no added sugar or fat in this fruity loaf – the sweetness
and moisture of the dried fruits are enough.
You will need a 20 cm (8 in) greased loaf tin or, if you wish, a round or square tin.

MAKES ABOUT 12 SLICES

10 dried pear halves

10 dried apricots

20 dried prunes

4 dried apple rings, halved

2 cups water

1 large banana

1 cup wholemeal self-raising flour

½ cup almond meal

¼ teaspoon cinnamon powder

1 teaspoon finely grated orange rind

Place the pears, apricots, prunes and apple rings in a saucepan with the water. Bring to the boil, cover and simmer for 5 minutes. Remove the apricots and apple rings from the pan and blend them to a purée with the cooking liquid and the banana. Place this purée in a large mixing bowl.

Preheat the oven to 180°C (350°F).

Mix the flour and almond meal with the fruit purée and gently stir in the cinnamon powder and orange rind. Spoon about a quarter of this into the cake tin. Top with half of the dried pear halves and then layer with another quarter of the cake preparation. Add a layer of prunes (use them all), and another quarter of the cake preparation. Lastly, add the remaining pears and top with the remaining cake preparation. Tap the tin to remove any air and bake in the preheated oven for 40 minutes. Allow to cool before unmoulding onto a rack.

Cool and store in an airtight container. This loaf keeps for 2–3 days.

French-style pancakes

French pancakes are called crēpes and are a very popular family dessert.
Serve them with freshly sliced fruits or with lemon and sugar.
You need a crēpe pan or a small non-stick frying pan about 18 cm (about 7 in) in diameter.

MAKES 6–8 CRÊPES

1 cup plain flour, sifted

a pinch of salt

1 teaspoon castor sugar

1 egg

about 1 cup milk

1 teaspoon peanut or canola oil

1 teaspoon butter

4 lemon wedges

Place the flour, salt and sugar in a mixing bowl. Make a well in the centre and pour in the egg and half of the milk. Using a whisk, first mix the egg and milk together, then gradually incorporate the flour, slowly adding the rest of the milk to form a smooth, thin mixture.

Strain the preparation through a fine strainer and refrigerate for at least 20 minutes or until required. If you are in a great rush, you can use it immediately, but the crēpes will not be as smooth.

Heat the oil and butter in a small non-stick pan or crēpe pan until it turns a light golden colour. Whisk this melted butter into the crēpe batter. Return the pan to a high heat and when it is hot, pour in enough mixture to coat the bottom of the pan. Twirl the pan in a smooth motion to form a thin, even crēpe. When the upper half of the crēpe starts to become dry and the lower half is golden brown, pick up the crēpe with a spatula and turn it quickly to cook the other side. After browning the second side, remove the crēpe and place it on a plate.

Without adding any more butter or oil to the pan, make the rest of the crēpes in the same way. If a crēpe begins to stick, wipe the pan with absorbent paper, melt a little butter in the pan and proceed.

Serve with wedges of lemon.

Pear Pudding

Enjoy this easy-to-prepare pudding either on its own or with the Sweet Creamy Topping on p. 182. You will need 4 individual buttered soufflé moulds and 4 pieces of foil to cover them.

SERVES 4

400 g (14 oz) can of pear halves in natural juice

1 large egg

1 tablespoon brown sugar

1 cup wholemeal self-raising flour

1 tablespoon melted butter (or margarine if you must)

1 tablespoon honey

1 tablespoon sultanas

Preheat the oven to 200°C (400°F).

Drain the pear halves, reserving the juice. Dice the pears.

In a medium bowl beat the egg and sugar for 2 minutes. Stir in the flour and pear juice alternately, half at a time. Lastly, stir in the melted butter and diced pears.

Spoon a quarter of the honey into each buttered soufflé mould. Sprinkle a quarter of the sultanas into each mould, then spoon the pudding preparation into moulds. Tap the moulds gently to get rid of any air bubbles and cover with foil. Place the moulds in a roasting tray. Add boiling water from the kettle to the tray to a level of 2 cm (¾ in) up the sides of the moulds. Carefully place the tray in the preheated oven and cook for 30 minutes.

Remove from the oven and peel back the foil. Run a thin blade around the edge of the moulds, turn out the puddings onto plates and serve.

Rice pudding & glacé pineapple & apricots

This is a satisfying family dessert. If you wish, replace the pineapple and apricot with other glacé fruits. Dried fruits work as well—just soak the fruits in warm water for about 1 hour before using.

SERVES ABOUT 6

1 cup short-grain rice

4 cups milk

3 tablespoons castor sugar

1 teaspoon grated orange zest

4 rings glacé pineapple, diced

4 pieces glacé apricots, diced

¼ cup pistachio nuts, finely chopped

Place the rice in a saucepan with a large quantity of cold water. Bring to the boil and boil for 4 minutes. Drain.

Bring the milk to the boil in a large saucepan. Add the rice, cover and simmer very gently for about 30 minutes, after which time the mixture should be creamy. Pay attention to the last few minutes of the cooking to ensure that the rice does not stick or burn.

Add the sugar, orange zest and glacé fruits. Stir well and cook for a further 2–3 minutes. Pour into a deep serving dish, sprinkle over the pistachio nuts and serve either hot or cold.

Baked nectarines with raspberries

In this easy, special-occasion dessert you can use peaches or red
plums instead of nectarines. Cook it in a large gratin or porcelain quiche dish.
It is also quite attractive cooked and served in individual dishes.

SERVES 4

¼ vanilla pod

1½ tablespoons castor sugar

about 16 raspberries

4 ripe nectarines, cut into eighths

2 tablespoons water

½ teaspoon rose water (optional)

a few chopped pistachio nuts or
1 tablespoon toasted, flaked
almonds (optional)

Preheat the oven to 220°C (450°F).

Halve the vanilla pod lengthwise and use your fingertips
to rub the sugar against the black seeds inside the pod.
This flavours the sugar.

Mash the raspberries with a third of the sugar and place
in a gratin dish. Arrange the nectarines on top,
overlapping the segments as you go. Sprinkle over the
water and rose water, and sprinkle with the remaining
castor sugar.

Bake in a preheated oven for about 20 minutes or until
the nectarines are soft and the edges lightly browned.
Sprinkle the pistachios or almonds on top and serve hot
or cold.

Apple tart on filo

Apple tart is the most popular dessert in bistros in France.
This is a very light version that uses filo pastry instead of the
traditional puff or shortcrust pastry.

SERVES 4

6 Granny Smith apples

2 tablespoons water

4 sheets filo pastry

a little peanut *or* walnut oil

1 tablespoon cream, low-fat
if you wish (optional)

1 tablespoon castor sugar

2 tablespoons apricot jam
or a little icing sugar

Peel, quarter and core two of the apples. Cook them with the water in a covered pan until soft. Mash the apple and allow to cool.

Peel, halve and core the remaining four apples, then cut them into 2 mm ($^1/_{10}$ in) slices.

Line a baking sheet with baking paper. Top with one sheet of filo pastry. Brush the pastry with a little oil and place a second sheet of pastry on top. Do likewise with the third and fourth sheets of pastry, brushing each sheet with oil as you go. Cut four rounds of pastry by placing a saucer on top of the pastry sheet and going around the edge of the saucer with the blade of a knife. Discard leftover pastry.

Preheat the oven to 200°C (400°F).

Stir cream into the cold apple purée and spread the purée over the pastry rounds. Place the apple slices on top of the purée, overlapping slightly so there are no gaps. You will probably have some left over – be as creative as you like with the pattern of the apple slices.

Sprinkle the top with castor sugar and cook in a hot oven for 15 minutes. The pastry should be crisp and the edges of the apple slightly browned. Before serving, brush the tops of the tarts with warm apricot jam or dust with icing sugar.

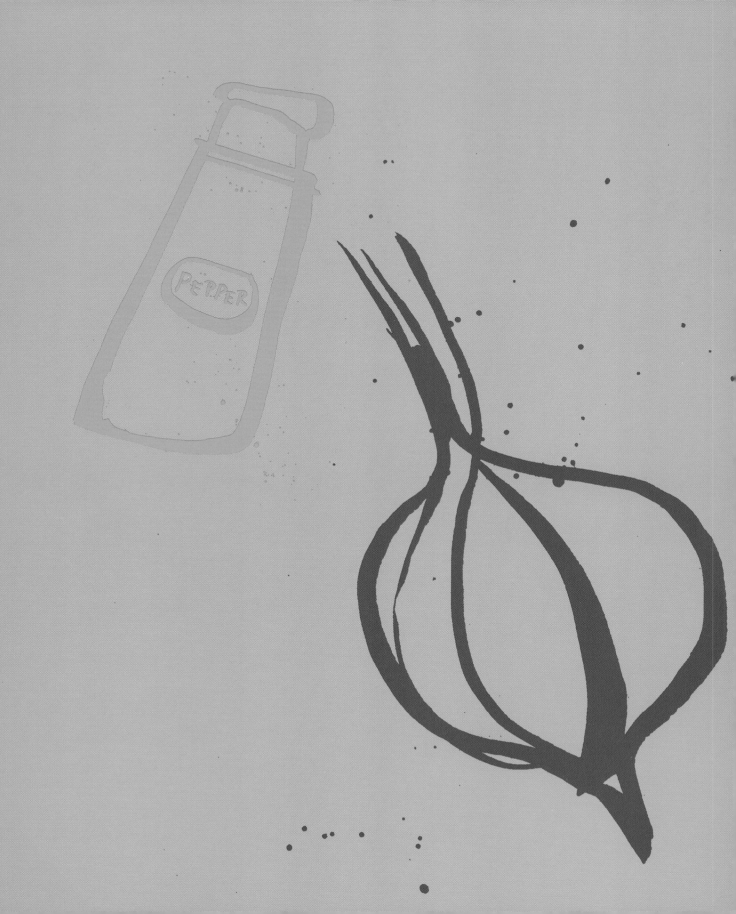

BASICS

In this final section I have given recipes for stocks and
sauces that you will find very useful. Stocks are used to
make tasty soups, casseroles and sauces, and a home-
made stock tastes so much better and is far healthier
than commercial ones. If you are using commercial
stocks, read the list of ingredients carefully before
buying as some contain monosodium glutamate (MSG)
or are very salty. The 'star' sauce in this book is the
Italian-style tomato sauce that I use in various recipes. It
is full of natural flavour, is low in fat and is easy to learn
to make. It can be adapted by adding herbs, spices
and vegetables. The other sauces are particularly useful
to those who love sauces and are on a low-fat diet.

chef's note

It is very useful to
keep home-made
stock in the freez[er]

Vegetable stock

This stock is especially handy for vegetarians to use instead of a chicken or veal stock. Cover and store in the refrigerator for 2 to 3 days or for up to one month in the freezer.

MAKES ABOUT 2 LITRES (8 CUPS)

½ tablespoon olive oil

1 brown onion, sliced

2 carrots, sliced

2 sticks celery, sliced

2 mushrooms, sliced (optional)

1 small leek, sliced

about 3 litres (12 cups) cold water

1 sprig of thyme

a few sprigs of parsley

½ clove

salt and freshly ground
   black pepper

Heat the oil in a non-stick pan and stir-fry the onion until lightly browned. Add the carrot, celery, mushrooms and leek and stir-fry for another 2 minutes before adding the water, thyme, parsley and clove. Season and simmer, uncovered, for 25 minutes.

Strain the stock and allow to cool before storing.

Chicken stock

A chicken stock is such a useful preparation for flavouring soups, sauces and stews. When your stock is made you can boil it down to a smaller quantity, cool and store in the refrigerator for 3–4 days or frozen for up to a month.

MAKES ABOUT 2 LITRES (8 CUPS)

approx. 1 kg (about 2 lb) chicken bones (carcass, neck, wings – skin and fat removed)

3 litres (12 cups) water

1 carrot, sliced

1 onion, sliced

1 stick celery or a piece of leek, sliced

a small pinch of salt

5 black peppercorns, crushed

1 clove

a few sprigs of parsley

a small sprig of thyme

½ bay leaf

Place the chicken bones and water in a large saucepan. Bring to the boil and skim with a spoon to remove any scum that floats to the surface. Add the carrot, onion, celery, salt, peppercorns, clove and herbs and simmer for about 1 hour, skimming the surface again if necessary. Strain the stock and discard the bones and vegetables. Allow to cool, remove any fat that forms at the surface and store.

Beef or veal stock

A stock is like an infusion, the idea being to obtain meat flavour from the bones. Depending on availability, use either veal or beef bones and ask your butcher to cut them into small pieces. This preparation takes about 3 hours, so plan ahead. Alternatively, use a commercial veal or beef stock.

MAKES 1 LITRE (4 CUPS)

2 kg (4 lb 4 oz) veal or beef bones

1 large brown onion, quartered

2 carrots, cut into bite-size pieces

2 sticks celery, cut into bite-size pieces

1 tablespoon peanut oil

1 clove

6 peppercorns, crushed

a few sprigs of parsley

1 bay leaf

2 sprigs of thyme

a pinch of salt

Preheat the oven to 250°C (500°F).

Place the bones, onion and carrots in a roasting tray and toss with the oil to coat. Place in the preheated oven and cook for 15–25 minutes to brown the bones and vegetables (avoid burning the vegetables). Remove from the oven and place the bones and vegetables, including the celery, into a stockpot or large saucepan, taking care to discard all the fat. Cover completely with cold water. Add the clove, peppercorns, parsley, bay leaf, thyme and salt. Bring to a simmer and cook for 3 hours, skimming the surface from time to time with a mesh spoon to remove the scum.

After 3 hours, strain the stock into a saucepan and boil to reduce to about 1 litre. Cool the stock, skim off any fat that rises to the surface and refrigerate or freeze. The stock keeps in the fridge for 3–4 days or up to 1 month in the freezer.

Fish stock

Made with fresh, cleaned fish bones, this flavoursome
liquid is handy to have for steaming or poaching fish fillets.
It is also used in the preparation of fish soups and sauces.

MAKES ABOUT 1 LITRE (4 CUPS)

500 g (about 1 lb) fresh fish bones such
as flathead, snapper or John Dory but
no freshwater fish or salmon

1 teaspoon peanut oil

1 small carrot, peeled and finely sliced

1 medium onion, peeled and finely sliced

1 stick celery, finely sliced

10 cm (4 in) piece of leek, finely sliced

a few sprigs of parsley

1 sprig of thyme

½ bay leaf

1 cup dry white wine

1½ litres (6 cups) water

salt and freshly ground black pepper

Wash the fish bones in water and remove any blood or
dark skin.

In a large non-stick saucepan, heat the oil and stir-fry
the vegetables for 5 minutes without browning. Add
the herbs, fish bones, wine and water. Season with a
little salt and pepper, bring to the boil and simmer for
20 minutes.

Strain the stock, pressing gently on the bones and
vegetables to extract the flavour. Return the stock to
the pan, bring to the boil and reduce to approximately
1 litre or less. The stock may be stored in a covered
container in the refrigerator for 2–3 days or frozen for
up to a month.

Peanut sauce

This sauce is the richest one in the book, and I recommend using it in moderation. It is a good accompaniment to steamed vegetables, rice, noodles and kebabs.

SERVES 4

2 cm (1 in) piece of ginger

½ small onion

1 clove garlic

¾ cup water

3 tablespoons desiccated coconut

1 teaspoon peanut oil

½ teaspoon curry powder

2 teaspoons fish sauce *or* soy sauce

1 ½ tablespoons crunchy peanut butter

½ teaspoon chilli paste

Blend the ginger, onion and garlic to a purée or, if you prefer, chop them finely.

Place the water in a saucepan with the coconut and bring to the boil for 10 seconds. Turn off the heat and allow the coconut to infuse.

In a small non-stick saucepan on low heat, gently fry the onion purée in oil for 5 minutes, stirring with a wooden spoon to prevent burning. Add the curry powder and fish sauce and stir well before adding the peanut butter and chilli paste.

Strain the coconut liquid into a bowl, pressing on the coconut to extract as much flavour as possible. Add the liquid to the peanut sauce and stir until the sauce is smooth. Cook on low heat for 2 minutes. It is now ready to serve.

Pesto

Pesto is more of a seasoning than a sauce. Its main ingredient is the very aromatic herb, basil, and 1 teaspoon of it is sufficient to season steamed vegetables or a portion of grilled fish or meat. Pesto is most commonly used with pasta. Store your pesto in a sealed jar in the refrigerator, and after each use, add a little olive oil to the jar to seal the pesto and prevent it from going off. Pesto keeps for up to two weeks in the fridge.

MAKES ABOUT 1 CUP

1 cup very fresh unblemished
basil leaves

2 tablespoons pinenuts

3 cloves garlic, peeled

2 tablespoons grated parmesan

2 or 3 tablespoons olive oil

Discard any blemished basil leaves. Wash the leaves, drain well and dry with a clean tea towel.

In a food processor, place the basil, pinenuts, garlic and parmesan. Blend to a paste. Slowly drizzle in the oil and blend until the mixture is well combined.

If not using immediately, cover with a film of olive oil and store in a sealed jar in the refrigerator.

Italian-style tomato sauce

The soft, sweet, rich texture of tomatoes makes them extremely versatile. This Italian-style tomato sauce can be used with pasta, fish, vegetables, meat, pancakes and pizzas. You can add your own personal touch at the end by adding a herb or spice of your choice, such as basil, tarragon, cummin or chilli. If you wish, double the quantities and freeze what is not required.

MAKES ABOUT 2 $\frac{1}{2}$ CUPS

about 1 kg (about 2 lb) medium-ripe tomatoes, cut into eighths

½ medium brown onion, peeled and diced

1 stick celery, from the heart, diced

1 medium carrot, peeled and diced

2 sprigs of parsley

1 sprig of thyme

1 clove garlic, crushed

1 teaspoon tomato paste

freshly ground black pepper

1 teaspoon olive oil (optional)

Place the tomatoes and other vegetables in a saucepan with the herbs, garlic, tomato paste and a little pepper. Cook, uncovered, on medium heat for 20 minutes.

Remove the herbs and pass the vegetables through a food mill or fine strainer. Check for seasoning and season if you wish. Stir in the oil before serving the sauce. It is best served warm.

chef's note

For the sauce a food mill gives the best results as it does not allow the tomato skins to go through. If you use a food processor or blender, pass the sauce through a fine strainer.

Curry & tomato sauce

Serve this sauce with steamed vegetables and rice. It is also good with grilled fish or meat.

SERVES ABOUT 4

½ brown onion

2 cm (1 in) piece of ginger

2 cloves garlic

2 teaspoons peanut oil

4 fennel seeds

10 cummin seeds

2 teaspoons curry powder

6 large tomatoes, seeded and finely chopped

2 tablespoons cooked lentils, from a can

½ cup hot water

¼ teaspoon chilli paste (optional)

1 tablespoon desiccated coconut *or* 1 tablespoon finely sliced coriander leaves (optional)

Peel the onion, ginger and garlic, then blend them together to a fine purée. Alternatively, chop finely.

In a medium non-stick saucepan place the oil, fennel seeds, cummin seeds and puréed onion, ginger and garlic. Cook on low heat for at least 5 minutes while stirring with a wooden spoon. If the ingredients start to burn add a tablespoon or two of water. Add the curry powder and stir for about 1 minute before adding the tomato and lentils. Bring to a simmer, add the hot water and cook on low heat for about 10 minutes, stirring occasionally.

Just before serving, stir in the chilli paste and desiccated coconut or coriander leaves if desired.

Many vegetable
can be cooked i
stock, blended i
a purée, and
served as a sauc
with fish, meat c
other vegetables

Red Capsicum Sauce

The smooth texture of cooked capsicum makes a delicious, strongly
flavoured sauce that is perfect for pasta, grilled fish or grilled vegetables.

MAKES ABOUT 2 CUPS

2 large red capsicums

1½ tablespoons olive oil

½ brown onion, chopped

2 large tomatoes, cut into eighths

1 stick celery, diced

1 clove garlic, chopped

1 sprig of thyme

a few sprigs of parsley

salt and freshly ground black pepper

Halve the capsicum, remove the seeds and cut each half into about 8 pieces.

Heat 1 tablespoon of oil in a non-stick pan and on low heat stir-fry the onion and capsicum for about 5 minutes.

Add the tomatoes, celery, garlic, thyme and parsley to the capsicum and season with a little salt and pepper. Cover and simmer for about 20 minutes. Remove the thyme and parsley and pass the sauce through a food mill, or blend to a purée and pass through a fine strainer. Check for seasoning and stir in the remaining oil before serving. If the sauce is too thick, dilute with some boiling water from the kettle.

Chilli dipping sauce

This spicy sauce is delicious with steamed vegetables, samosas and food served in filo pastry. Consume it in moderation as it is fairly salty, sweet and spicy.

SERVES 4

2 tablespoons water

1 tablespoon sugar

½ tablespoon white-wine vinegar

1 tablespoon fish sauce

½ clove garlic, finely chopped

¼ teaspoon hot chilli paste (sambal oelek)

1 tablespoon roasted peanuts, chopped

In a saucepan bring the water and sugar to a simmer and boil for 2 minutes. Allow to cool.

Mix in the vinegar, fish sauce, garlic, chilli paste and peanuts and serve.

Spicy pea & carrot sauce

This lovely sauce is very low in fat and full of goodness.
Serve it with grilled, steamed or pan-fried meat or fish, or with vegetables.

SERVES 4–6

1 teaspoon peanut oil

1/4 brown onion, finely chopped

1/4 teaspoon curry powder

1 large tomato, diced

1 medium carrot, finely sliced

1 1/2 cups chicken (p. 204) *or*
vegetable stock (p. 203)

1/2 cup shelled peas

a pinch of chilli pepper

salt and freshly ground black pepper

Heat the oil in a non-stick saucepan and fry the onion and curry powder for 3 minutes. Add the tomato and stir well. Add the carrot and chicken stock, and bring to the boil. Add the peas and season with chilli pepper and a little salt and pepper. Cook for about 15 minutes until the vegetables are tender.

Blend the vegetables and liquid to a smooth sauce and strain if you wish. If the sauce is too thick, dilute with a little hot water from the kettle.

Menus for Special Occasions

Mother's Day

Broccoli Soup with a Hint of Curry (p. 44)

Pan-fried Salmon with Dill and Vegetables (p. 127)

Pear Pudding (p. 195)

Father's Day

Chicken in Red-Wine Sauce with Carrots (p. 151)

Green Salad with Walnut Dressing (p. 56)

Apple Tart on Filo (p. 198)

Christmas Day

Smoked Salmon and Avocado Parcels (p. 79)

Roast Christmas Turkey with Bread and Orange Stuffing (p. 154–55)

Green Salad with Walnut Dressing (p. 56)

Your Favourite Christmas Pudding *or* Peach, Mango and Berry Salad in Pawpaw (p. 187)

A Romantic Dinner

Asparagus Soup (p. 44)

Salmon Tartlets on Filo (p. 137)

Williams Pears and Passionfruit Salad (p. 183)

A Fish Dinner

Scallops, Asparagus and Mesclun Salad (p. 141)

Fish and Prawn Soup with Fennel (p. 49)

Fresh Mango

A Vegetarian Dinner

Cauliflower and Mushroom Curry (p. 118)

Tomato and Spicy Bean Tartlets on Filo (p. 93)

Fresh Fruit Platter with Two Berry Sauces (p. 184)

A Light Alfresco Lunch

Salade Niçoise (p. 61)

Peach, Mango and Berry Fruit Salad in Pawpaw (p. 187)

An Italian Meal

Focaccia with Olives and Thyme (p. 72)

Risotto with Chicken and Vegetables (p. 108)

Seasonal Fruits with Fresh Ricotta Cheese

A Chinese Meal

Stir-fried Vegetables with Roast Pork (p. 176)

Spicy Stir-fried Prawns with Bok Choy (p. 138)

Seasonal Fruits

An Indian Meal

Vegetable Samosas (p. 76)

Curried Flathead with Coriander and Celery (p. 136)

Dates and Orange on Yoghurt (p. 182)

A French Meal

Artichokes Provençale (p. 120)

Grilled Loin of Lamb Provençale (p. 170)

Fresh Berries

One-dish Dinners

Serve any of these with a salad.

Minestrone Soup (p. 47)

Vegetarian Pizza (p. 88)

Couscous with Grilled Lamb Kebabs (p. 175)

Tagliatelle Marinara with Vegetables (p. 132)

Paella (p. 109)

Singapore-style Noodles (p. 105)

Risotto with Chicken and Vegetables (p. 108)

CONVERSION CHARTS

Symbols used in this book

ml = millilitre

mm = millimetre

cm = centimetre

L = litre

oz = ounce

lb = pound

in = inches

Volume Measurements (workable approximates)

Spoon and cup measurements used in this book are metric.

1 metric teaspoon =   5 ml

$\frac{1}{2}$ metric tablespoon = 10 ml

1 metric tablespoon =   20 ml

1 US teaspoon =   5 ml

$\frac{1}{2}$ US tablespoon =   7.5 ml

1 US tablespoon =   15 ml

$\frac{1}{4}$ metric cup =   62.5 ml =   about 2 oz

$\frac{1}{2}$ metric cup =   125 ml =   about 4 oz

1 metric cup =   250 ml =   about 8 oz

4 metric cups =   l litre

Note: The US cup is a bit smaller than a metric cup.

Weight Measurements (workable approximates)

15 g = $\frac{1}{2}$ oz

30 g = 1 oz

60 g = 2 oz

90 g = 3 oz

120 g = 4 oz

150 g = 5 oz

200 g = 7 oz

250 g = 9 oz

300 g = 11 oz

400 g = 14 oz

500 g = about 1 lb

1 kg = 2.2 lb

Measures (workable approximates)

1 cm = $\frac{1}{3}$ in

2 cm = $\frac{3}{4}$ in

2.5 cm = 1 in

5 cm = 2 in

10 cm = 4 in

20 cm = 8 in

Oven Temperatures (workable approximates)

100°C	= 210°F	Very slow	
125°C	= 240°F	Very slow	
150°C	= 300°F	Slow	Thermostat 1
180°C	= 350°F	Moderate	Thermostat 4
200°C	= 400°F	Moderately hot	Thermostat 6
220°C	= 450°F	Hot	Thermostat 7
250°C	= 500°F	Very hot	Thermostat 9

Glossary

abalone mushroom see mushroom

al dente An Italian expression, meaning 'to the tooth', usually used in reference to the cooking of pasta to a degree that offers a little resistance when bitten into, but is not soft.

baste (to) To spoon or brush food, usually roasts, with liquid or fat to keep the meat moist.

bean sprouts The sprout of the mung bean, very popular in Asian cooking. It is usually sold by weight or packets in markets and foodstores.

blanch (to) To plunge food for a brief time into boiling water in order to precook or soften it.

bok choy A very popular variety of small Chinese cabbage. It is usually sold in bunches of three heads. Available from many greengrocers and most Asian foodstores.

Chinese broccoli A green leafy Chinese vegetable used extensively in Asian cuisine, especially in stir-fries and soups. Both the stems and leaves of the vegetable can be eaten.

Chinese cabbage Also known as *wong nga bak*. There are many varieties available, and the one most commonly used looks like an elongated European cabbage. They have pale yellow to pale green tightly bunched leaves.

chop (to) To cut ingredients into tiny pieces. Herbs are best chopped using a 20 cm (8 in) or longer chef's knife. For casserole dishes such as a curry, you can use a food processor to chop up ingredients such as onion and ginger.

coriander Also known as cilantro, especially in the USA. This is a herb with small leaves and a strong, pungent flavour. The leaves are used in Asian and Middle-Eastern cooking, and the roots are used as part of a spice mixture in Thai curries. Available from most greengrocers.

couscous A form of pasta made from coarse wheat semolina. Available from most supermarkets and gourmet food stores and usually comes in 500 g (1 lb) packs. Couscous is a staple food in North African countries and is served with vegetables, fish and meat.

dice (to) To cut food into 1 cm ($1/3$ in) cubes, especially vegetables. To dice, the food is first sliced, then cut into small sticks (batons) and finally cut across into small squares.

dried bean-curd A by-product of the soybean, and popular in Asian vegetarian cooking. Available in the refrigerated section at Asian foodstores. It comes in air-tight plastic packs of 4 or 6 squares.

egg noodles These come in many varieties – thin, thick, fresh or dried. The recipes in the book usually call for Hokkien noodles or egg noodles, and they are readily available from the refrigerated section of Chinese grocers. Reconstitute dried noodles in boiling water for about 3 minutes or until they are soft, then proceed with the recipe.

filo pastry A very thin Greek pastry that is relatively low in fat and easy to use for wrapping around foods. Available from Greek gourmet foodstores and in the refrigerated section of most supermarkets.

fish sauce A salty, strong-flavoured Asian sauce popular in Thai and Vietnamese cooking. It is made from fish extract and used as a seasoning. The salt content varies from brand to brand, so use it in moderation and taste the dish as you are cooking.

flageolet beans A variety of small French kidney beans that are pale green to creamy white in colour, and rarely available fresh in Australia. They can be purchased dried or canned from gourmet foodstores.

focaccia A flat Italian bread available from Italian gourmet shops and some bakers. A recipe for focaccia is provided on page 72.

glacé fruit Also called candied fruit. Fruit preserved in a sugar syrup; usually used in desserts.

glaze (to) To brush pastry or finished desserts with jam, fat, milk or egg yolk to give them a shiny finish.

grill (to) Refers to either cooking under an oven grill or on a grill on top of the stove or barbecue. Top-of-the-stove grills are usually made of cast-iron.

harissa A hot chilli paste made from dried chillies, garlic, cummin and other spices. It is popular in North African countries where it is used to flavour soups, stews and casseroles, and couscous. Available in jars from gourmet foodstores and supermarkets. Substitute with an Asian-style chilli paste or sambal oelek.

marinate (to) To coat or cover meat, fish or poultry with a seasoning of liquids, spices and herbs.

Mesclun salad The French name for a mix of small green salad leaves. Available from better greengrocers and some supermarkets.

mushroom, abalone A medium-sized mushroom with a subtle flavour, popular in Chinese cuisine. Available fresh from some greengrocers.

mushroom, cloud ear Also called *wun yee* or wood ear mushroom. A Chinese mushroom, sold dried in Chinese grocers. When dry, it is black and curly and looks like seaweed. To use, soak in hot water until the mushroom is soft and has increased in size. It has a crunchy, bland flavour.

oyster sauce A salty, strongly flavoured Asian sauce made from an extract of oysters. If possible, select a brand without MSG.

poach (to) To gently cook food, covered, in a hot or simmering liquid.

polenta A coarse cornmeal popular in Italy. It is cooked in water until it forms a paste and then baked or pan-fried and served with meat, fish or vegetables. A recipe is provided on page 90.

ratatouille A dish of mixed cooked vegetables, including tomato, eggplant, capsicum, zucchini, olive oil and herbs. Popular in the south of France.

reduce (to)   To diminish the quantity of a liquid or sauce by boiling it in order to obtain a smaller quantity, greater concentration of flavour and thicker consistency.

refresh (to)   To cool food by holding it under cold running water. Usually for the purpose of arresting the cooking process.

rice, Arborio   A short-grain Italian rice used for risotto. Available from department stores, some supermarkets and Italian foodstores.

rice, basmati   An aromatic long-grain rice that releases a floral smell during cooking and a fine texture. Usually served with curries and Indian food.

sambal oelek   A hot chilli paste used in Asian cooking. Available in jars from supermarkets and Asian foodstores.

sesame oil   A very flavoursome oil made from sesame seeds. It can be overpowering, so use it in small quantities.

shaoshing wine   A Chinese wine made from rice and used in small quantities in Asian cooking for flavouring. It has an alcohol content of 16 per cent. Available from Chinese foodstores and keeps well for months in the pantry.

simmer (to)   To cook food in a liquid that is just below boiling point, when the bubbles are just about to break on the surface.

small sticks   Also known as batons. Usually referring to the way vegetables are cut. The vegetable, for example, a carrot, is first cut into 5 or 6 cm (about 2 in) lengths, which are then sliced lengthwise (approx. 5 mm thick ($^1/_5$ in) and then cut lengthwise again into 5 mm ($^1/_5$ in) sticks.

soy sauce   There are many varieties of soy sauce and some are saltier than others. Made from an extract of soybeans, wheat flour and other seasonings.

steam (to)   Usually refers to the cooking of food in a steamer but can also refer to cooking by steam in a small amount of liquid in a covered saucepan.

stir-fry (to)   To cook food in a little oil while stirring and tossing to stop the food from sticking or burning. When stir-frying vegetables it is sometimes necessary to add a little water down the side of the wok or pan to stop the vegetables from burning.

tahini   A flavoursome paste made from sesame seeds and used as a spread. It is an ingredient of hummus, the Middle-Eastern dip made with chickpeas.

tamarind   A small, tropical, acidic fruit shaped like a broad bean. It is available as a liquid concentrate or dried from Asian foodstores. When using the dried form, soak a small piece in some hot water. Drain after 10 minutes and strain off the juice. Use the juice and discard the solids.

wun yee   see mushroom, cloud ear

iNdex

Numerals in **bold** indicate colour plates.